Beckles Willson

The Tenth Island

Being some account of Newfoundland, its people, its politics, its problems, and its

peculiarities

Beckles Willson

The Tenth Island
Being some account of Newfoundland, its people, its politics, its problems, and its peculiarities

ISBN/EAN: 9783744726504

Printed in Europe, USA, Canada, Australia, Japan

Cover: Foto ©ninafisch / pixelio.de

More available books at **www.hansebooks.com**

The Tenth Island

BEING SOME ACCOUNT OF NEWFOUNDLAND,
ITS PEOPLE, ITS POLITICS, ITS PROBLEMS,
AND ITS PECULIARITIES

BY

BECKLES WILLSON

WITH AN INTRODUCTION BY
THE RT. HON. SIR WILLIAM WHITEWAY, K.C.M.G.
PREMIER OF THE COLONY

AND SOME REMARKS ON NEWFOUNDLAND AND THE NAVY BY
LORD CHARLES BERESFORD, C.B.

LONDON
GRANT RICHARDS
9 HENRIETTA STREET, COVENT GARDEN
1897

Upon a recent re-perusal of Mr Rudyard Kipling's "Song of the English," I was not a little struck by the absence therein of any reference to the "Tenth Island." Happening, shortly thereafter, to discuss the poet with a Newfoundlander, Mr George F. Bearn, we both speculated upon the omission. I suggested, playfully of course, that he should write to Mr Kipling asking him for an explanation. My suggestion was adopted.

"I really must point out to you," wrote Mr Bearn, "how greatly disappointed we Newfoundlanders have been at your ignoring us in your stirring and eloquent 'Song of the English.' You speak of Montreal, of Auckland, of Victoria, of Halifax: and yet seem to pass purposely by that deserted and ruined citadel of the first-born of England's colonies, least blessed and most banned by the Imperial Mother.

"Read our history, sir; read Lord Dufferin's speech at the Cabot celebrations the other day at Bristol, and see if we have not been loyal and long-suffering. Come amongst us and see if we to-day are less loyal or less ready to shed our blood for the land of our fathers. We too have our message to the Imperial Mother, although the poet of the Empire has not thought fit to transcribe it.

"We have long been accustomed to have our geography

ignored and our politics and our resources misunderstood; but I beg of you, sir, to repair the injustice you have done to our loyalty."

To this letter Mr Kipling responded as follows:—

"North End House,
"Rottingdean.

"Dear Sir,—What can I say in reply to your letter of the 13th, except that it is rather a large order to compress allusions to the whole of our Empire into two hundred lines of alleged verse. And when it comes to my sins of omission—well, I ought to have included Perth, West Australia; Dunedin of the Southern Island, N.Z.; the West Indies, and a few other places.

"But indeed I am not unmindful of Newfoundland. Perhaps I may know more about it than you think; and certainly no man in his senses ever doubted the loyalty of the senior colony. We can leave that, I think, to the Yankees, who seem to take comfort from inventing curious fictions of that nature.

"However, when and if there is another edition of my verses, I will do my best to put in Newfoundland's voice also, but the task is not a pleasant one. If I leave out all reference, I am taxed with 'injustice.' If I make a pointed reference, as I did in 'Our Lady of the Snows,' I am, to put it mildly, supposed to be scaring away immigrants by misrepresenting the climate of the dominion.

"But we will make a bargain. I will put in a four-line

verse among 'The Song of the Cities,' if you, on your part, will drop, and influence other people to drop, allusions to the 'loyalty' of the 'colonies.' In the first place, I dislike the word 'colonies,' and, if you look through my verses, you will find I very seldom use it. It is out of date and misleading, besides being provincial. In the second place, there is no need to talk of 'loyalty' among white men—that is to say, races speaking the English tongue, with a high birth-rate and a low murder-rate, living quietly under laws which are neither bought nor sold. That is one of the things we all take for granted—because the Empire is Us—We ourselves; and for the white man to explain that he is loyal is about as unnecessary as for a respectable woman to volunteer the fact that she is chaste.

"Like yourself, I am a colonial in that I was born in Bombay, but it has never occurred to me to say that I am 'loyal,' because, like you, I am a white man, and—one can't step out of one's skin.

"Very sincerely yours,

"RUDYARD KIPLING."

A FORE-WORD

By Sir William Vallance Whiteway, K.C.M.G.

At this critical juncture in our history the good opinion of the English-speaking world is the matter of the most vital importance to us, an opinion based not upon such comparative trivialities as our social refinement or the breadth of our public spirit, but upon the honesty and good-heartedness of our people and the capabilities of our country.

I am a sanguine believer in the resources of Newfoundland, although it has been kept in its present backward state for a period of four hundred years. Efforts were systematically made to prevent the colony being settled, so that the fisheries should be carried on there by those resident in the old country. And in this manner the fisheries were prosecuted until early in the present century. It will hardly be believed, nevertheless it is a fact, that when I myself emigrated from Newfoundland, about fifty years ago, there was only one important road in the country: that to Portugal Cove. Now we have a network of roads reaching to all the principal and a majority of the smaller towns and settlements in the country — in fact, thousands of miles — and our roads are, as a rule, good. Such is the remark of strangers visiting us. If our present population were relegated to the condition existing fifty years ago, when the hardest ship's-biscuit, fish, Hamburg butter, and pork was the food, scarcely ever a potato or vegetable on the table, when cabbage was an imported luxury almost unknown, when a path over the hills was the road around Conception Bay, what we have accomplished would be more vividly seen. Our colony has spent a great deal which is represented in assets. St John's alone has cost upwards of £400,000 in widening, making, and straightening its streets. In Harbour Grace and Carbonicre a very large sum has been expended from time to time for a like purpose. We cannot have these advantages without paying for them. There are forty-nine lighthouses and fog alarms, thirteen hundred and thirty-five miles of telegraph line and cable, the dry dock, all the public buildings, Government House, the Colonial Building, the hospitals and asylums for the lunatic and the poor, the post offices, court-houses, penitentiary and gaols, and an immense mileage of roads, a great portion of which has been made from money borrowed on capital account. Then we have the s.s. *Fiona*, costing £8000, public wharves, and some breakwaters. We have six hundred miles of railway across the island, yet our population is only 210,000 people; wherefore I say these are great works to be achieved by so small a number. It has been said that Englishmen at home hardly appreciate the work we have had to do in the colonies, and in this colony in particular. Yet I could point to hundreds who have made their money in the colony I represent, and come home to spend it. Were the money made in the colonies spent in the colonies, one of them, at least, would be in a different position to-day. Nevertheless, we do not desire that a man should not spend where he pleases the money he has made; but we do desire that when we are asked to give large amounts for the defence of the Empire you should consider these few facts. When muscle is required and men are required, and when England may be in difficulties, Newfoundland will not be backward in shedding its blood for her. I remember that the initiatory step in the long series of developments which have made England to-day the supreme ruler of the seas, was one with which my colony of Newfoundland was associated. The fishing-vessels on its coast, and the thousands and tens of thousands of men engaged in that great industry, were then forming the foundation of England's present supremacy, and they stand to-day ready at any moment of England's peril to come forward to her aid.

But what has been secured in times past by the bravery of the soldier and the sailor has, unfortunately, been disposed of by the diplomatist. We have suffered in all times past, and we are struggling to-day under treaties— I may call them infamous treaties — which surrender to France two small islands off our coast, and convey to the French fishermen, in the most ambiguous language, what we claim to be a concurrent right of fishing along part of the shore of our own island, but what they claim to be an exclusive right, and are exercising as an exclusive right. It seems difficult to believe that not long ago, when endeavouring to arrange for the construction of a railroad across the island, it was contended by the French that we could not even erect a railway station on what is termed the Treaty Coast — and we were precluded for years by the Government of this Mother Country from building that road! During the present year we shall have completed that road; but I may almost say that we have secured the railway station surreptitiously. We hesitated about giving any information whatever as to what we were doing until we had the road and the jetty constructed, lest the French would protest that they would interfere with their fish on the coast. These are facts, and facts which are operating so prejudicially as to retard the progress which we ought to make as the oldest colony of Her Majesty's Empire.

The question of the future of our growing population has, for some time, engaged the earnest attention of all thoughtful men in this country, and has been the subject of serious solicitude. The fisheries being our main resource, and to a large extent the only dependence of the people, those periodic partial failures which are incident to such pursuits continue to be attended with recurring visitations of pauperism, and there seems no remedy to be found for this condition of things but that which may lie in varied and extensive pursuits.

This reflection would apply with force to the present population, but when we contemplate it in relation to our increasing numbers, the necessity of dealing with the subject urgently presses itself on our consideration.

Our fisheries have no doubt increased, but not in a measure corresponding to our increase of population. And even though they were capable of being further expanded, that object would be largely neutralised by the decline in price which follows from a large catch, as no increase of markets can be found to give remunerative returns for an augmented supply.

It is evident, therefore, that no material increase of means is to be looked for from our fisheries, and that we must direct our attention to other sources to meet the growing requirements of the country. Our mining industry may now be regarded as an established fact. Large areas of geological formation similar to that in which the mines are being successfully worked are known to exist, and there is every reason to believe from recent explorations that a great amount of wealth in copper and other ores is waiting the application of enterprise and capital to bring them into profitable use. Our agricultural industry, though prosecuted to a valuable extent, is yet susceptible of very enlarged development.

Vast stretches of agricultural land, extending from Trinity Bay north, along the heads of Bonavista Bay, Gander Bay, and Exploits River, as well as on the West Coast, need only the employment of well-directed labour to convert them into means of independent support for thousands of the population.

We have in the capital a large market for agricultural produce and live stock, which at present is mainly supplied from abroad; and, as an illustration of what might be done by the cultivation of the land when a market is within reach, we have the fact that amongst the most prosperous of our labouring people are those who live by the land in the vicinity of St John's, though the average conditions of fertility are far below those which exist in the interior of the island. There are indications, moreover, leading to the conclusion that we shall hereafter be more dependent than before on home supply of live stock, for in those places from which we have hitherto received our meat supplies attention is being given to the English market, which is supposed to offer better prospects, and an advanced value may therefore be reasonably anticipated.

With an improved market on the spot, the inquiry is further suggested whether this colony should not become an exporter of live stock to England; and we have little difficulty in affirming this position. For grazing purposes we have large tracts that, we believe, cannot be surpassed in British North America; and when we regard our proximity to England, and the all-important consideration of a short voyage for live stock, the advantages we possess in this connection are too manifest to be subject of question or argument.

To practical persons the minor criticisms that are made in this book are matters of supreme insignificance. On the other hand, it does matter to the outside world who may propose to have dealings with us that we are a "hospitable, amiable people," that our language is beautiful, that our mineral wealth is real and extensive, and our agricultural resources many and promising. These chapters carry with them all the weight of competent and disinterested authority. Much of their matter I cannot undertake either to defend or refute. It is, as one critic has observed, "mere *obiter dicta*, sayings by the way, humorous comments on our necessarily somewhat narrow existence; and, as for the much-resented reflections upon some of our insular customs, though unflattering, they can hardly be called unkind."

We have passed through an ordeal which is unprecedented in the history of any colony. The fire of 1892 laid a great portion of the city in ashes. The failure of the Banks and of many mercantile firms, the poor Labrador fishery of last years, and the unfortunate result of the present seal fishery, present a sad picture; but there are yet good grounds for substantial hope and we should not be cast down. We know the fisheries are ever varying, but they will never fail. The mining prospects are bright. The surplus population must look more to the land; and I have every confidence, if we sink these petty party squabbles when we have to meet outside difficulties, and there is a cessation of these defamatory telegrams and newspaper articles as regards the people and the country—communications in the shape of sensational telegrams which are a disgrace to the senders are being sent abroad, to the great damage of the country — and if we cultivate a spirit of patriotism, good days are in store for us, for I have every confidence in the future of the country. Her fisheries, her minerals, her timber and agricultural lands bespeak a bright future for our Island Home.

It has been too often the case that a class of persons who have not even seen the Island nor had any knowledge of its inhabitants or its institutions have rushed into the press to air their crude ideas and express decided opinions upon the subject of which they know nothing, and so heartburnings are caused and injuries inflicted, not probably intended by the writers, but yet the consequence of their rashness. Anything which tends to make the Island better known, and, if better known, it must make it more favourably known, has my cordial support. Newfoundland has been my adopted country for upwards of half-a-century during thirty-nine years of which I have taken an active part in the management of its public affairs; and I think I may be excused if I seize this opportunity of calling attention to the progress which has been made, for it is now a source of much gratification to me that I have been permitted to assist in bringing about the improvements which have been accomplished.

I entertain little doubt that if the reader's thoughts are turned, or are likely to be turned,

A FORE-WORD   xix

towards colonial enterprise, he will carry from the perusal of this book the fixed impression of a country full of great possibilities, teeming with a vast almost untouched mineral wealth, and the home of a brave and vigorous people.

THE TENTH ISLAND

CHAPTER I

NEWFOUNDLAND is not on the visiting-list of countries. It is a *terra incognita* to tourists. Albeit at the very portal of the Western Continent, hundreds of thousands annually pass her by—this Cinderella of the Colonies, who, somewhat lean and rather ragged, as yet, sits patiently in her corner of a hemisphere.

Newfoundland is our first-born, our oldest colony. Here were made the beginnings of England's empire, and the Newfoundland fishermen were the early core and backbone of her navy. But England has always been a stern parent to her children; it therefore follows that Avalon has suffered most injustice and neglect. Her sisters have flaunted her; and all her relations have heaped calumny and cod-fish upon her headlands. If she opened her mouth to speak, they have thrust a cod-fish down her throat. Did she smile? then they taunted her with her fogs.

If you were to consult a chart of the ten largest islands on the world's surface, you could place your finger on one and almost be conscious of its heat, you could touch another and feel its cold: one would inevitably suggest beauty, another ugliness; this would be distinguished for its history, that for the density of its population; this would be rich and powerful, another poor and weak. An island is a standing invitation to the imagination — and, in fancy at least, mankind is for ever sailing to an island. May not the political future of the world be said to lie with islands? After England it may be, thousands of years hence, the Empire of New Zealand, of Ceylon, of Borneo, of Jamaica; but if there be truth in that dictum which declares that "the law of the world's progress is an advance from the warmer to the colder latitudes," destiny must have much in store for that island which occupies a similar geographical relation to the New World that England occupies to Europe, and Japan to Asia.

Putting aside all material, political, and historical considerations, and regarding size only, you would begin with Australia and end with Newfoundland. It is not only because it is the first of England's colonies, nor because its fisheries were the foundation of England's naval greatness, nor because during two centuries it contributed many millions of pounds sterling to our national wealth, nor because of its bearing on international relations, that this Tenth Island is to me the most curiously fascinating of them all. It is fascinating, too, because of the peculiar progress an isolated Anglo-Saxon-Celtic race is making to-day from rudeness and ignorance and ugliness to culture and enlightenment and beauty.

Newfoundland's vicissitudes have been numerous and picturesque, and she has been, in Lord Salisbury's phrase, the "sport of historic misfortunes." The island is the possessor of a romantic history, at which it might be as well to glance before entering on a description of it as it is to-day.

The earliest known inhabitants were the Beothuks—a numerous and powerful race, who may have been allied to the North American Indians, or have been, on the other hand, a distinct and older race who at some date lost in antiquity migrated to the island.

When John Cabot came upon these shores in 1497 the Beothuks were at the height of their numbers and prosperity. The island possessed an abundance of wild game; its shores and innumerable lakes swarmed with cod, trout, and salmon; countless herds of reindeer roamed over the interior; and the thick forests afforded the aborigines a grateful hermitage when they ceased from their annual wanderings. Physically they were a well-developed race, "ingenious and of quick intelligence, gentle in their manners, tractable, and not indisposed to friendly intercourse with the pale-face." They inhabited this fine rude country in perfect peace and goodwill, practising no agriculture, attired in the skins of beasts, happy in the chase, in their camp fires, and in their simple loves and pleasures. In all of these respects the Beothuks must have borne a striking resemblance to the earlier inhabitants of another rude island in a slightly less southerly latitude, which has by centuries of cultivation become one of the gardens of the world, and to which about a third of the civilised world at present owns sovereign allegiance.

But the doom of the Beothuks was sealed when the white men came. The same contest which was carried on in the mainland between Europeans and savages was carried on in Newfoundland. It was little to be expected that the first white trappers, hunters, and fishermen would have much toleration for aborigines who interfered with their pursuits. The utmost brutality was evinced by the whites, and responded to with interest by the Beothuks. But when the latter vowed "war to the knife," the white invader declared war to the pistol and carbine; and the fire-arms of the white man soon began to wreak a terrible destruction on the natives of the island, thinning out their numbers, and driving them into the interior. If a whole tribe can be said to have died of fright and despair, it can truly be said of the Beothuks. For in this shelter, their spirit crushed and their most powerful chiefs slain, and fearful of venturing again to the coast, they gradually decayed, being thenceforward seldom seen by the eye of the white man. Their last stand seems to have been made at Red Indian Lake: and here the bones of their ultimate hundreds only yesterday strewed the ground or are yet embedded in the mould — here the Beothuks perished to a man. In 1828 a missionary, journeying to their settlement with Bible and cross in hand, found the ruins of their wigwams, fragments of their canoes, remnants of their dresses, and the graves of their dead; but all around, as far as the eye could pierce, was pervaded by the silence and sombreness of the tomb. What remain of the Beothuks to-day are a few skulls, a skeleton, some bones, and a collection of their implements which I saw in the Museum at St John's.

Long before Sir Humphrey Gilbert, in 1537, thought of colonising the island, the great value and importance of the Newfoundland fisheries were appreciated; and an interest existed which could not have been surpassed had the Grand Banks been instead the mines of Golconda and Peru. One must remember that the sixteenth century was the golden age of fish. England, like the rest of Europe, was a Roman Catholic country, and the fasts and ordinances of the Church were respected everywhere by the masses. Fishing was not only profitable, but, carried on with enterprise, was a sure road to great wealth. The monopoly of the herring fisheries by the Dutch was one of the causes of that country's mediæval opulence.

The tidings, therefore, that a watery tract had been discovered off the shores of Cabot's New-Found-Land which bore within its bosom millions of shoals of the largest and finest of that highly-prized fish, the cod, was received with wonder and delight. Not only rich mariners, but richer nobles, took part in the new fishing emprise; and soon all Europe rang with the fame of Newfoundland, as all its marts groaned beneath countless quintals of its cod.

Yet England was not the first to avail herself of this new treasure ground. As early as 1504 the hardy and adventurous fishermen of Brittany and Normandy were engaged off the Newfoundland shores; and the Basque, Portuguese, and Spanish mariners came closely in their wake, even making settlement on the shore. And then, by-and-by the English fishermen came to claim their own, in small numbers at first, but increasing until they had outdone their rivals, profiting thereby to such purpose that Sir Walter Raleigh was able to declare in Parliament that the Newfoundland fishery was the "stay and support of the West counties of England."

Thus the zeal and ardour which first led men westward in large numbers, and even led them to erect dwellings on the land, was born of a desire to supply cod-fish to Europe; and the diet of the Church was to influence more than any other factor the destiny of a continent.

It is a curious reflection that when Sir Humphrey Gilbert first set out to colonise Newfoundland, France and Spain were dividing among themselves the whole of the New World; and England, who was subsequently to be mistress of a continent, did not then possess a square foot of American territory. But Gilbert's expedition, although undertaken under royal auspices, and under the direct patronage of Elizabeth, was foredoomed to failure. The English did not then understand those minor arts of colonisation which every petty trader in Africa has at his finger ends to-day: and which, indeed, of themselves make of colonisation an art. Their supplies gave out, their shelter and clothing was insufficient; but, before Sir Humphrey Gilbert sank beneath the billows on his return home to England, he had the satisfaction of planting the Royal Standard on the site of the future city of St John's, and declaring Newfoundland the possession of his monarch, the Virgin Queen.

Twenty-six years later came Guy's colony, a scheme promoted by John Guy, a merchant of Bristol, who set forth the attractions and possibilities of the island in a pamphlet which commanded such attention that a company was formed, settlers enrolled, a vessel chartered, Guy appointed Governor, and sail set for Newfoundland. Guy's plantation was, however, unsuccessful, owing chiefly, it is said, to the piracy then prevailing. Nothing daunted, in 1623, three years after the sailing of the *Mayflower*, there came Lord Baltimore, and a cargo of superior emigrants, with a patent conveying to him the whole Southern peninsula, which he forthwith named Avalon. He built a splendid mansion at Ferryland, and set his energies to work to make the colony prosperous.

But England was new at Empire in those days, and allowed the French, who had got a strong foothold on the mainland, to so harass him and his colony that Baltimore at length returned home, leaving his colonists to fight and shift for themselves; and they have been, alas! fighting and shifting ever since.

Even the novelty of the Mother Country's first steps in Empire-founding will scarcely excuse the great blot in the history of her relations with her first New World Colony. For

THE TENTH ISLAND

it was about this time that she began that policy of allowing the slender flicker which some of her best and bravest blood were trying to fan into a flame, to be almost totally extinguished.

For more than a century and a half the settlement of a great and fertile island, one-sixth larger than Ireland, was discouraged, not merely morally, but through system and statute; and no endeavour spared by a large and influential class of persons to both blacken the fame of Newfoundland and to keep it a mere fishing-station for the fishermen of Devon. The island became thenceforth a temporary habitat for the mariners of the West Countree. They went out in their ships each year, and at the close of the season they returned. Newfoundland represented nothing more to the merchants and shipowners of England than a barren clod of earth—or, at most, a certain limited line of shore—and, to be frank, to them it is little more to-day. Their business was then, and is now, with fish and the money they make out of the fishermen.

These "merchant-adventurers," as they were called, having resolved that the fish wealth of Newfoundland should pass into West Country coffers, rather than it should be diverted, even in part, to residents of a new colony, were able to influence successive English Governments to the passage of unjust and deleterious laws which came perilously near throttling the colony in the first days following its birth. These laws prohibited anyone to go out to Newfoundland as a settler, and "ordained that all fishermen should return to England at the close of each fishing season." Masters of vessels were required to give bonds in £100, binding them to return each year with such persons as they took out. Settlement within six miles of the coast was prohibited under heavy penalties; nor could one cultivate or enclose the smallest piece of ground without licence, which was rarely granted.

But for these vicious and selfish enactments, which, in spite of their occasional evasion by hardy spirits, effectually thwarted the fair growth of the colony, can it be doubted that Newfoundland to-day would contain large cities and smiling estates — that the towns of St John's, Placentia, and Harbour Grace would resemble in size and character Boston, Portland, and Halifax; and that the island, instead of being merely a coast-line—a collection of fishing villages—would have its interior densely populated with a healthy, contented, and loyal race?

The battle between the earlier colonists and their oppressors lasted until about eighty years ago, when the English Government awoke to

THE TENTH ISLAND

a sense of its disgrace, and the last of the noxious statutes was repealed. In 1729, however, England had appointed a Governor and given formal recognition to the island as a British colony. At that time the population only numbered 6000 persons; but the number is large when one considers the obstacles and oppression they had to face. Courts of Justice were established; the navigation laws were extended to the island, and a collector and comptroller of customs appointed. Freedom of religion was proclaimed, and the existing deplorable system of religious persecution abated. Immigrants began to find their way to those shores; yet it was not until 1820 that the restrictions on building houses and cultivating ground were entirely abolished. Even then, and to this day, as the shadow of the system which had gone before, there remained in the mind of Europe the image of a fog-bound rocky isle, devoid alike of foliage, sunshine, and fertility; and existing only for the drying of the fish entrapped in the wild and dreary waste of waters. Since then a new battle has been waged by the unfortunate Newfoundlander—a battle for the recognition of its forests, its fertile prairies, its blue skies, its majestic mountain scenery, the intelligence and culture of its inhabitants, and the island's progress generally. These claims, coming from Newfoundlanders themselves, have been received by an incredulous universe without enthusiasm. It is still regarded by many as a "land of cod-fish and dogs, fogs and bogs." Yet Newfoundland has not been without her share of attention. The monstrous treaties enacted between Great Britain and France on the subject of her territory have been brought up more than once in the eye of the world in the light of a burning question; and having been brought up and made to pose picturesquely for a period, are retired at the expense of England's honour, to the shame of her statesmen, and to the despair of her first-born and harshly-used colony.

CHAPTER II

CONSIDERING the popular ignorance of its aspect and capacities, the Tenth Island should be distant at least ten thousand miles. It must be a matter of some surprise to discover how near Newfoundland is to the British Isles. Speaking for myself, a voyager to a land wrapped almost in fable, I could scarcely realise it. A passage by a fast steamer of three and a half days is all that separates Queenstown from St John's. Approaching the harbour of the colonial capital I fancied, as I stood in the stern of the vessel, and scented the breeze, that I was being pursued by the vivid odours of Irish peat. And what a new area this proximity to England may open up for this colony! Why should she not become one of the highways of Empire to the West? The great British North American — nay, the great Imperial dream of the future is Newfoundland received into the bosom of the other Confederated provinces: a fast alternative steamship service from Milford Haven to Bonavista Bay accomplishing the journey in three days; a Pullman express train across the island; and so *via* packet to Sydney, and from thence to Quebec and Montreal by rail. In such a fashion, not only could the Canadian metropolis be reached in a matter of five or six days, but the abbreviated ocean passage would tempt thousands to travel to the New World who shrink now from lengthier communion with the sea. But I shall have occasion to speak of this Fast Line project hereafter.

Just now we are approaching St John's. No one would suspect that behind these dark frowning cliffs, these miles on miles of rocky heights, whose bold promontories and headlands have been sculptured fantastically by the action of the waves, there lie towns and villages and a habitable country. Newfoundland presents a stern exterior to the world; and this perhaps is not least among the causes which have retarded her advancement into the good graces of mankind. Dull lowering cliffs warn off the intruder, fogs in summer and ice in winter zealously guard its shores — how irresistibly it all reminds one of the fairy tale in which the dragons and their treasure so prominently figure!

A brown mountain cleaves for us abruptly in twain, and with this great towering rocky mass on our right and on our left, we enter what is called the Narrows. The aspect is not unlike Gibraltar, especially on the left, but where are the fortifications?

A fellow-passenger pointed out to me, indeed,

the ruins of a barracks on the slope. The main structure and the outhouses had lingered on, untenanted for twenty years. Once or twice, so my informant told me, a homeless fisherman, or one of those waifs to be found in every community, had been driven to a scant refuge within those walls; and there is even the story of a man found mysteriously drowned in a cistern beneath the flooring. But the regiment of red-coats had departed; and the populace took only a melancholy interest in the fate of their former habitation. Then a few years ago the great fire came along and left the establishment a mass of smoking ruins.

"I shall never forget," quoth my Newfoundlander, "the spectacle that day in 1871 of Her Majesty's soldiers and their officers filing slowly down Signal Hill on their way to the ship which was to bear them away for ever. Gladstone will always be remembered in this country for that act. It seemed as if the last tie was being broken. We felt, too, that St John's was the key, not only to this island, but to the whole continent — not even Quebec is so impregnable as this would be with a moderately-equipped battery. We ourselves offered to pay; but, of course, the English Ministry would not hear of it. 'It wasn't a question of money.' Then, if it wasn't, good God, what was it? And philosophise as we would, with the breaking up of that garrison every man of us felt that the colony, which had never ascended many, had gone down another step in the world."

Truth to tell, it strikes even the unpractised eye as difficult to over-rate the strategic importance of these heights of St John's in the event of hostile attack. The city is placed almost in the heart of the Peninsula of Avalon, the nearest point to Europe, with a port the most secure perhaps in the world; how easily might St John's be made the Gibraltar and Sebastopol of America. A few thousand pounds and a regiment or so of British soldiers and the thing is done. Wherefore it is impossible to believe that the Home Government was not thoroughly aware of the importance of maintaining an effective garrison, from one standpoint; and of the eminent undesirability of doing so if regarded from another —*i.e.* as a temptation to the colonists toward self-assertion and even belligerency in their attitude towards their aggressors. The fact of the matter is this — the Newfoundlander is, in his attitude towards the outside world, the most helpless creature in the universe. Docility having thus been inculcated by nature, it has been the policy of successive British administrators and Colonial governors, in view of his unparalleled grievances, to continue him in that blissful state. This ingenious policy has

THE TENTH ISLAND 17

not only evacuated the garrison, and dismantled the batteries, as evincing a bad example to the colonists, but has repeatedly discountenanced, and so far successfully, the establishment of any volunteer militia force for the protection of the island.

I think I do well, at the outset, to present the reflections which were uppermost in my thoughts at the moment of my first glimpse of the island — for if I believe truly there is no property of similar value and extent, not merely in our Empire, but in the universe, so absolutely undefended and unprotected, there is no similar property which must inevitably, if things continue as they are, stand in need of such defence and protection. I have heard said, and with much truth, that this island is the one appanage of the British Crown which would have the least chance of successfully alienating itself politically from the Empire. But supposing that the attitude of the Mother Country amounts at length to a virtual abandonment of her interests in the colony—a solitary interest, for all one is able to discern—into whose clutches will the island, naturally, and as if by reversion, fall? The French have long claimed partial sovereignty over the territory, and the guns of the last fort they have remaining to them in North America are within sounding distance. It is likely that the Americans would be heartily pleased to see rapacious John Bull displaced by the "lawful owners of Newfoundland." The Newfoundlanders, it seems to me, though as stalwart and brave as Poles, would, like Poland, have to suffer territorial dismemberment, if not complete conquest. In view of the French claims, and England's apathy and acquiescence, no other result can happen. It would not be a case of war; but of simple acquisition. England, if not diplomatically, has long ago, morally, abandoned the island to the French. Her ludicrous abdication of her rights in consequence of aggression and threats has been all but complete; and if she had intended that the retention of the island should cost the life of even a single English soldier, she would have made war long ago.

It is while I am surveying Signal Hill and its departed glory that the city of St John's bursts out of its hiding-place. It is on the right bank of the little oval harbour—a slim town of obviously greater length than breadth, yet looking compact enough as it sits smiling on the slopes of a hill with a forest of shipping at its feet. The object which most effectually strikes the eye is the Roman Catholic Cathedral with its twin towers, which, being posed on the town's highest land elevation, lend it the graceful aspect which it would otherwise lack. This

THE TENTH ISLAND

Cathedral alone of the chief churches escaped the great fire of 1892.

"D'ye ken for why?" inquired the cabman of extraordinary appearance, and of still more extraordinary dialect, who drove me from the wharf to my hotel. "'Twas the stones were a' fetched from Ireland, sor."

This, *en passant*, was my first experience of the Newfoundland dialect—one of the most marvellous composites on earth. To the home Briton it cannot fail to be most diverting. For the first five minutes you are confident you are conversing with an Irishman—the next five minutes you are highly amused at your mistake. The man is a Scot—probably from Skye or Shetland or some remote community you have never visited. The next five minutes you ask him how long he has been from Devonshire. Sometimes he brings all three nationalities to bear on you in one sentence, as did a Placentia man with whom I climbed a hill. When we had reached the summit,

"Aweel, sor, ye're afther being athwart the rudge," he said.

"Athwart the rudge" is pure West Country, as Mr Blackmore can testify.

It is amazing how quickly St John's has arisen from her ashes. The town has been the prey of many conflagrations. In 1816 three distinct fires occurred, the first of which, in

February, consumed 120 houses and left 1500 people homeless; the second, in November, destroyed 130 houses; and the third, in the same month, reduced a large part of the business portion of the city to ashes. But even this memorial year of fires was as nothing compared to 1846, when 12,000 persons were burnt out of house and home and three-quarters of St John's was a mass of smoking ruins. But the conflagration of July 8th, 1892, was the greatest in the history of the colony. Fully one half of the town was consumed, including the Church of England Cathedral, the work of Sir Gilbert Scott and the pride of St John's, with a loss of three millions sterling. The truth is, the town is set in a trough; and the wind sweeps through it incessantly winter and summer. Repeated trials have caused the St John's firemen to become among the most expert I have ever beheld (I was shown how they get their engines and apparatus into the street seven seconds from the sounding of the alarm), but the utmost celerity and heroism fight an uneven battle when they fight with the wind. In addition, most of the houses—even the mansions of the best class—are built of wood.

In contemplating the general architecture of the capital, one is led to speculate on the different aspect it would have presented

THE TENTH ISLAND 21

had the conditions of its settlement and the system of its commerce been different. For nearly four hundred years the dwellings of rich Newfoundlanders—men who made their fortunes out of the industry of the island—have graced London, the Clyde, Bristol, Plymouth, and many provincial towns. The millions which in England have been but as a drop in the bucket of the general opulence, would have erected stately mansions and designed elegant enclosures. The cod-fish and the seal would have made of St John's what the fox and the beaver have in part made of Montreal, what the pine and the cedar have made of the New Brunswick capital. But were St John's to resemble other cities in its appointments, half its interest, for me, at least, would evaporate. It is what the town will become, in a mental comparison of its present appearance to that it will have in the course of the next twenty years, that constitutes its chief attraction. The incessant process of building, consequent upon the recent devastation, and the manner in which private dwellings are built close up to the line of pavement, with little or no suggestion of trees or gardens—this is hardly calculated to give one an impression of municipal beauty or of municipal pride. At present the citizen generally is dead to beauty, and uniformly without imagination. On the other hand, St John's is well policed, well watered, lighted, and sanitated, and the telephone is in every office and even every sitting-room.

The many thoroughfares of St John's (which, as I have said, is set on the side of a not too gently undulating hill) are very steep, very wide, and very long. One of them, Gower Street, is famed, and I am ready to believe justly, for having seventy hills. Some of them are so steep that it is a marvel how the horses manage to ascend them in winter time, when the ground is frozen hard and slippery; but they are of a tough, wiry breed, these horses of St John's, and a level country would probably puzzle them. At the top of Cochrane Street, on the ridge of the hill, the flag of England flies over Government House: a large plain building enclosed within spacious grounds; while close at hand, to the westward, is the Parliament building, a low stone structure beautified by a fine pillared portico. I observed from the first a monument at the top of Cochrane Street, a stone's-throw away from where I had taken up my quarters, and was impertinent enough to suggest that this was probably erected to the memory of that excellent Governor and zealous innovator, Sir Thomas Cochrane, who ruled over the colony some seventy years ago.

But I was mistaken. This pretentious shaft,

THE TENTH ISLAND 23

exalted in the most prominent portion of the city, was to the memory of some humble individual who had rescued another humble person from drowning, a private act of valour; whose memory, but for this memorial, would probably live enshrined only in the hearts of that humble person's relations and friends. During the fortnight I spent in St John's I was unable to pick out a more apt and striking illustration of the utter lack of imagination and perspective which distinguishes the inhabitants than this monument standing there in its lonely significance before Government House. But the chrysalis already shows signs of bursting its shell, for one of the natives said to me—

"I am beginning to think that it was a mistake to allow that poor fellow's friends to choose that site. It looks terribly parochial. Sure, it's where the statue of the Queen herself ought to stand."

Although there are numerous thoroughfares in the capital, there is only one street, and that is Water Street. I am moderately familiar with a hundred of the world's cities: and I have spent many hours in contemplating their meanness, their opulence, their beauties, and their uglinesses, but I am ready to back Water Street of the fish capital to be the most amazing of them all. Though ill-paved, ill-kept, and running parallel to the wharves, it attracts all the commerce and fashion of the town. If you can imagine Lower Thames Street, Billingsgate, with Oxford Street and Pall Mall all bundled together, with a bit of the Mile End Road thrown in, you will form a fair conception of this singular avenue. Possibly the St John's people will one day arrive at a sense of its incongruity, and contrive that a new fashionable shopping street shall be instituted in the more select portion of the town. I spoke of Water Street attracting all the commerce and fashion of the town. If Newfoundland is St John's, then St John's is Water Street. The great merchants here are the descendants and legatees of the English merchant-adventurers of ancient days. Their establishments are huge general stores of the Hudson's Bay Company pattern, devoid of pretensions to beauty, either within or without. To the eye accustomed to the order and neatness of Whiteley's or Wanamaker's shops, there seems, probably on the surface only, an absence of form and method. Slippers are mysteriously dragged out of biscuit boxes, and barrels conspicuously labelled flour are found upon inspection, and often to the obvious astonishment of the clerk, to contain corsets. The interior of several such establishments I visited struck me more as factories or warehouses than as shops. Yet so they have been conducted almost for centuries, doling out to the fisherman the necessaries of life (and a few luxuries) and receiving in return his quintals of cod. Undoubtedly the business transacted is immense. One firm turns over to the value of some three million dollars annually. A million and a half is handed over the counters of another.

At the farthest extremity of Water Street, at the head of the harbour, is perhaps the chief of St John's public works—the dry dock, which is capable of accommodating all but the very largest steamers afloat. It is 600 feet long, 83 feet broad, with a depth of 25 feet on its sill at low water. It was opened in 1884, and cost nearly 600,000 dollars. Chief among the architectural beauties of the city are the two Cathedrals, with the Bishop's palace, St Bonaventure's College, and a Convent. The capital also boasts a public Museum, in which are stored and arranged a very creditable collection of minerals, relics, and stuffed animals pertaining to the island. The curator and official geologist, Mr Howley (the brother of the Archbishop), I found to be an acute and highly capable gentleman.

The Newfoundlander is very proud of his Newfoundland dog; and it is a pity that the admirable local museum does not possess one or two specimens—stuffed. For there are no live ones—at least very few.

I was told that when the Prince of Wales was here in 1860, a superb specimen was presented to His Royal Highness; but even then the best breeders and fanciers had removed to England. Newfoundland itself can take little credit for the superb and now almost extinct animal associated with her name. It was a happy accident—a cross, I believe, between a mastiff and a spaniel or setter.

But it was not about dogs, but about goats, that the capital was exercised just prior to my visit. The goat is a virtuous quadruped. He cleaves to the poor, and he has a habit of increasing. He has also other habits — such as roaming at large, and taking an unfair advantage of unoffending pedestrians. So that now the Municipal Council of St John's have fallen foul of this animal, and shipped him off into the wildernesses of the interior, indemnifying the owners at 3 dols. a head. Several sportsmen returning from the Exploits river region report meeting a shivering herd of these unfortunate creatures there, who, should they survive the winter, will be added to the list of game which inhabit the island.

CHAPTER III

POLITICS run high in Newfoundland, and they run all the time in St John's. "If Newfoundland ever comes into the Dominion," the late Sir John Macdonald used to say, "we shall never be able to find places enough for them. They eat too much fish."

The lamented Premier was wrong as to the diet of the Newfoundlanders, but right as to the number of place-hunters. There is more fish eaten in St Giles parish on a Saturday night than there is in a week in St John's. The Newfoundlander of the outports—the name given to every coast settlement outside the capital—lives much more largely on salt pork or dried beef than on fish. There are two parties—the Liberals and Conservatives—and I have the authority of that genial and accomplished judge and historian of Newfoundland, Mr Prowse, for saying that so far as the character of their public men is concerned, there is "not a pin to choose between them."

On the great national issues, such as that of the French Shore question and the St Pierre smuggling question, they are as one man. And, very curiously, it was the Conservatives, or

Merchants' party, that granted the boon of manhood suffrage to the island at large.

But all political parties, whatever their deviations and subsequent character, have fundamental principles. To arrive at the fundamental principles of the Merchants' party one must go back to that period, extending over three centuries, when settlement was systematically discouraged for the benefit of Bristol, Plymouth, and Barnstaple.

The profits still, in the main, find their way to the old country—the funds of the local capitalists go to England or the United States. The colony is sucked dry. Local capital is rarely invested here: the great field for local philanthropy in the way of public charities, public institutions, and public churches is unoccupied. Rich deposits, according to the testimony of experts, of copper, of iron, of coal, and of gold stand begging for capital simply because the foreign capitalists are inclined to rate the country no better than the home capitalists rate it.

In the course of a talk I had with a member of the Merchants' party, he stated his attitude fervently and succinctly.

"Newfoundland began with fish, and we must go on with fish. It is good enough for us. If we want to invest in mines, there are plenty elsewhere. They may be no better or no worse than Newfoundland mines; but there must be no clashing of interests."

The merchants, however, although holding the wealth of the country, are a small section numerically. Therefore, the spokesmen of the party to which they belong do not make too much of this argument. They even take it upon themselves to deny it. But the great fact remains that the great railway just being completed across Newfoundland was built in the very teeth of the Merchants' party, and that it is being operated by a Montreal capitalist.

The merchants had formerly great political power and influence with the masses of the fishermen; but they lost this when they conferred upon them the boon of the secret ballot. The masses now vote fearlessly for whom they choose — and naturally against their masters. Party feeling is apparently very bitter, but I strongly suspect much of this bitterness is on the surface. But, real or apparent, it is sedulously fostered by the three daily papers of St John's, two of which belong to the Opposition. For whatever scurrilities and discreditable personalities the Western American press is famed, I have yet to see the prints, either in Texas, Arizona, or Colorado, which can at all approach the delicious blackguardism of those three St John's newspapers.

Every day when I took up my *Herald* or

Daily News I would find sentences directed against the Government, in the following amiable vein:—

"The Whiteway party is a shameless gang of boodlers, rogues, and jobbers. The citizens are sick of them and their ringleader."

"The generous and peace-loving citizens of Newfoundland are at the mercy of moral cut-throats and assassins. But the time of retribution is at hand; and the knees of Morris, Bond, and Whiteway were seen to tremble with a consciousness of guilt as they strolled along Water Street yesterday."

Yet the *Herald*, by the way, is edited by the very talented young gentleman who acts as correspondent for the London *Times* and leading American newspapers, and thus may be said to stand sponsor for the colony to the outside world. The *Telegram*, being the Whiteway organ, naturally voices the virtues of those in office; while attributing at the same the worst motives to their antagonists.

One of my first calls was upon the Premier of the colony, Sir William Whiteway. The name of this gentleman is not altogether unfamiliar in England. For thirty years he has been a factor in the island's politics. He is rather a handsome, bearded man, whom I might readily have mistaken for Sir Walter Besant had I seen him coming down Chancery Lane into the

Strand. He is not a native of Newfoundland, but was born in Devonshire. It must not be forgotten that Newfoundland itself is largely an offshoot of Devon. I could detect nothing of the professional politician about Sir William. He talked at first very keenly about shooting cariboo and catching trout. He is a keen sportsman; and his sunny personality made me comprehend at once the hold he has on the masses of the islanders—a hold that no amount of calumny can loosen.

"What are the colony's prospects, Sir William?" I asked.

"We have emerged from the shadow," he replied. "The crisis is over, and signs of prosperity are on every hand. Newfoundland is about to be opened up to the world. Ten years ago we were a coast line—now we are a country; and the railway across the island, which for twenty years I have striven for, is now within thirty miles of completion. Our mines of copper, of iron, of coal, and of gold are forcing themselves on the attention of Europe. Oil has been found in great quantities, and is now being worked. Everything, especially the railway, fills us with confidence."

Knowing that the Premier had been, in principle at least, a firm believer in union with Canada, "What about confederation, Sir William?" I asked.

"That is shelved for the present. We wanted to come in two years ago, but the Canadian Government would not agree to our terms."

"What were those terms?" I asked.

"Their assumption of our public debt of 16,000,000 dollars, contracted chiefly in building our great railway. They were ready to assume 10,000,000 dollars only, and the negotiations fell through. Had Sir Charles Tupper, instead of Sir Mackenzie Bowell, been at the head of affairs, we might have been a part of Canada to-day."

"Do the masses of Newfoundland favour confederation?"

"No; I do not think they do. As yet the majority is against it; but the benefits resulting from the confederation are so apparent to the thinking men, that that majority is dwindling daily. Understand, it has never been made a party question. When our credit was ruined in 1894, we took the issue in our own hands. It was either confederation, reversion to a Crown colony, or a European loan. We secured the loan, and the crisis passed. I may add the bonds of the colony are now at par."

The Premier has one sore spot: it is his intense dislike and distrust of newspapers. Some of his experiences have been so exceptional that one can readily comprehend and even condone his bitterness. Considering the sources of Newfoundland news which has hitherto been sent

THE TENTH ISLAND 33

to the English newspapers, I promised the Premier to record the following utterance:—

"There are," he said, "five species of statement regarding this colony against which I wish to warn the British reader. They are the absurdly exaggerated, the utterly ridiculous, the genial fabrication, the ignorant falsehood, and the malicious lie. As much harm is done this colony through mistaken zeal as through malice."

The leader of the Opposition—*i.e.* the Conservatives—is Mr Morine, an undeniably able lawyer—the legal ferret of Newfoundland—whose governing purpose seems to lie in the direction of a betterment of his political fortunes. He emigrated a few years ago from Halifax, and has since tried in vain to enter Dominion politics, under the wing of Sir Charles Tupper. This goes far to explain the bitterness of the term "alien" as applied to him, for the Newfoundlander is nothing if not parochial. With a rude, ignorant population to appeal to, Mr Morine is not always the Mr Morine of his own drawing-room; and even the niceties of political etiquette are not always rigidly adhered to. The thing for the stranger to do is to know the situation, and then he might be at Exeter Hall for anything he would find startling or offensive.

"You're a low, dirty blackguard," vociferated the Opposition leader to a man who interrupted him at a meeting I attended in the British Hall

C

"You're a low blackguard yourself," retorted the interrupter. Both statements were thought sufficiently interesting to applaud.

Before this meeting, Mr Morine told me that he intended bringing a charge against the Whiteway Government of giving away two and a half million acres of public land to the contractor who had built the railway. An elector had said to him that if this charge were true, he himself would take down his sealing gun and shoot Sir William Whiteway and Mr Bond.

The charge was brought, but it fell rather flat.

It was plain these men were fishermen, not land-lubbers. Sir William might give half the island in fee simple to the Emperor of China: it was all the same to them.

The facts are, however, that land in the interior is worth about thirty cents an acre. Any settler can go and procure uncleared land in any quantities at this figure. Mr Reid, the contractor, agrees to operate the new road for ten years, and to take land in lieu of cash. The cost of operating the line is estimated at 100,000 dols. a year. If anyone with an earth-hunger wants land to-morrow, Mr Reid will dispose of any part of his property on precisely the same terms as he received it.

Mr Bond is the Colonial Secretary, an office corresponding to the American Secretary of State. He, with Mr Morris and Mr Horwood, is among the youngest and most cultured of the governing class. He is the gentleman who came to England and negotiated the loan of some 3,000,000 dols. when the colony was in sore straits in 1895—just after the failure of its Banks. There is no doubt that this Bank crash was due to gross mismanagement; but, in spite of repeated charges and counter-charges, I do not believe that any public officials were criminally culpable. Yet I should not be surprised to discover that "Who broke the Banks?" were yet made an election cry at the date of the next quadrennial election.

My impression of all the Government officials —the so-called Whitewayites—is that they are ambitious men, who, nevertheless, have the interests of the colony at heart, who are doubtless bent on doing their duty, but who suffer much from an anomalous system of conducting public affairs, as well as from the absence of a more numerically equal Opposition. This anomalous system is the result of the sparse settlement of the island, which leaves work usually undertaken by local boards to the member for the district, who himself makes grants out of the public moneys. The Opposition availed themselves of this in 1895, to bring charges of corruption, which temporarily unseated the Whitewayites. Albeit, they soon returned to office, in the language of the judiciary, "without a stain on their characters."

Commerce in the colony learnt a salutary lesson from the commercial *debâcle* of 1894. The chief cause of that disaster was beyond question the "vicious and dangerous system of banking on which for years the business of the country had been conducted." Before the crash came it was the easiest thing in the world to obtain credit, even to the extent of hundreds of thousands of dollars, and naturally advantage was taken of this by firms who were hopelessly entangled in debt. An inflation of trade was the result: and the capital of two Banks soon exhausted. Yet business went on, and the community suspected nothing, until one morning the Union and Commercial Banks stopped payment. As their notes constituted the entire currency of the colony and were held by everybody—high and low—a panic was inevitable. There being no money to purchase goods, shops and places of sale were deserted, and shortly afterwards began to announce their insolvency. But the worst was to come. A run on the Savings' Bank—a Government institution—began, and then the moral and pecuniary depression of the colony was at its lowest ebb. But the situation, sad as it was, had been inevitable for years: and even now there was supplied the element of humour. No sooner did the news of the island's distresses reach Halifax and Montreal than several young men began flying across intervening land and sea, in a terrible anxiety to reach the fish capital ahead of their rivals. In a comparatively few hours after the "Black Monday" crash the citizens were startled to see the shutters of no less than three hitherto untenanted offices down and placards severally inscribed:

   BANK OF MONTREAL.
  NOW OPEN FOR BUSINESS.
  NOTES DISCOUNTED HERE.

   BANK OF HALIFAX.
    NOW OPEN.
  MORTGAGES TRANSACTED.

   BANK OF NOVA SCOTIA.
   DEPOSITS RECEIVED.
    ETC., ETC.

The condition of the two defunct Banks was, on examination, found to be hopeless. The only excuse that can possibly be alleged for their directors is that, like Micawber, they were waiting for "something to turn up"—some rise in the fish markets, or some other lucky chance which would lift them out of the mire of insolvency. While they waited the Government was induced to lend them money out of the Savings' Bank, little suspecting, of course, their true status.

The three before-mentioned Canadian Banks have now probably replaced permanently the defunct institutions, the Savings' Bank has again been rendered safe by Government, credit has been restored, and a blow has been dealt the pernicious credit system, by the improved banking methods introduced by the Canadian Banks.

After each visit I paid to the Provincial building, I remarked a numerous body of fishermen and nondescripts loitering in the vicinity. They were dressed in every conceivable shape and style of garment, with some quite inconceivable details as to fit, colour, and patch, with tanned, whiskered countenances, and chewing tobacco, for the most part. These, I was informed, were influential electors come up to demand work and favours. Rough, hardy, and unlettered mariners these, who had smelt of politics from afar, and seemed to have acquired a zest for the banquet. And so they came up, and chewed and spat on the Ionic porticoes and exchanged stories of marine adventure, patiently waiting until they could unfold their grievances or their demands to the "skipper," as Sir William is called. For they are "afther having nothing else in the world to do."

As I called to pay my respects at Government House I was struck by the beauty of the country about me, as far as eye could reach. Who would have believed this was Newfoundland? The roll-

THE TENTH ISLAND 39

ing lands were bathed in the sunshine of Italy, and studded with trees and houses, and intersected with picturesque brooks and fine roads.

Pursuing my path, I caught a glimpse by the wayside of a finely-built, ruddy, white-bearded gentleman in a tweed cap toiling resolutely with a shovel.

It was the Governor, Sir Herbert Murray, K.C.B.

CHAPTER IV

PAROCHIAL as it is, the Tenth Island boasts an Upper Ten. The judges, lawyers, merchants, and higher grade public officials constitute the aristocracy, if so it can be called, of the colony. These are so inter-married and connected socially or commercially that, as was observed at the time of the Bank crash in 1894, "to touch one reaches all." But this is only true in part and of late, for the merchant, like the merchant-adventurer, even when he condescended to reside in the colony, which, in truth, was not often, held strictly aloof from the rest of the community. The reason is not difficult to seek. Newfoundland was merely a means to an end: and he distrusted the ability of her inhabitants to support that distinction with equanimity. No country feels flattered at being regarded as a means to an end. He credited them with designs on his purse in the shape of railway communications, general enlightenment, and the fostering of industries not connected with his own. Little by little there has developed a class, small indeed as yet, of the well-to-do who look at Newfoundland as their home and that of their children; and with the spread of this class the public spirit and well-being of the capital and of the island will advance by leaps and bounds.

Of course all society in St John's revolves about Government House; but the functions which have their centre here are unfortunately the tamest possible affairs, and by no means calculated to allay that thirst for luxury and excitement which youth and beauty even in St John's experience. Government House, in however remote a colony, should be a great and splendid refining influence—a sort of branch court of Buckingham Palace or Windsor Castle, where the latest topics of art, and politics, literature, fashion and the drama might be interchanged; and where even the most untravelled and insular might snatch something of that grace of culture, that gospel of good-breeding which make London and Paris delightful places to live in. But to accomplish this, ever so slightly, requires money and—a hostess. Fancy Sir Francis and Lady Jeune set down for five years in St John's. Figure to yourself this pair—chosen at random—the dual personification of hospitality, tact, and, I might add, munificence—how they would galvanise the social energies of the colony—arouse its best and most admirable qualities in a way that religion itself is powerless to do. For, the reader must be informed that although Government House is the nominal high temple of society, its altar is really in the Cathedral. To this altar — and when the pulpit is occupied by youthful and comely vicars and curates, to say nothing of bishops, it is no mean shrine—the belle of St John's brings her most spiritual thoughts and her prettiest frocks. St John's, barring a few Scotch and Asiatic communities — is the most religious town on earth. There is more religion here to the square inch than in any place I have ever visited.

It is a curious fact that when any society, through lack of exhilarating outlook, is driven to prey upon itself, it invariably turns wondrously religious. In its faith, and in the beautiful visions which that faith conjures up, it appears to find all the solace and entertainment it requires. For a long time, when the country is barren and the horizon dull, it refuses any bliss that is not born of religion. It was so, and is so largely yet, in Scotland, but not so much as some of its novelists would have us believe. But let the hand of man wrest from Nature her charms, let smiling fields and green pastures appear on her bosom, and men reach Art by the pathway of Nature. Banish both Art and the beauties of Nature, and the world is a prison-house. Newfoundland has probably produced hundreds of painters and poets and musicians; but, unfortunately, their talents have all been stifled by the spirit of their environment. It has produced thousands of beautiful women and graceful men; but the spell of the cod-fish is over all, and boorishness and uncomeliness soon supplant beauty and grace. I visited the studio of a native artist, a lady, who had just returned after many years' absence in Scotland—and I must say this lady's work delighted me by its freshness and skill. But she seemed to shrink from native subjects as a pre-Raphaelite would shrink from a stereotype; yet surely a great opportunity awaits her in portraying the singularly beautiful scenery and picturesque human types of her native land.

The two denominations—that of the Church of England and the Roman Catholics—run each other hard for precedence in the capital, as in the island; but I believe there is comparatively little proselytism. The clergy have charge of the entire educational system of the island, all attempts to establish an undenominational establishment having failed. More than that, they are entrusted with whatever form of secular entertainment or diversion with which even the better classes beguile themselves. St John's possesses no theatre; but it is doubtless unaware of any deprivation: for one of the most delightful charms of its people is their total inability to perceive that their city is any wise lacking in culture, beauty, or equipment. I do not think I have ever known a society freer from introspection and fault-finding. It is only among the very young that a spirit of unrest occasionally creeps out; but age and a perpetual consciousness of futility soon represses this spirit, if it does not lead them to join the larger life of Canada or the United States.

Here then we have the prospect of a Celtic-Saxon community, strong of mind, body, and moral and spiritual purpose, at the eve of the twentieth century slowly developing itself according to the canons of the past. Mails are seldom, and correspondents rare. Immigration having ceased many years ago, the ties with the outside world are slender. Even when they exist, the Newfoundlander seems to be conscious of an inferiority which he cannot explain, and which makes him shrink within himself. The outports turn to St John's for social comfort and inspiration, and the capital feasts upon itself. The result is a social—nay, even a moral —dyspepsia. In an English provincial town one occasionally encounters a great deal of gossip, of scandal, of petty slander. It is worse in the colonies; but in St John's, I am grieved to say, this spirit achieves a triumph. On the day following my arrival, the *Daily News* contained the following advertisement in a prominent place:—

THE TENTH ISLAND

"As a large number of people in this city are given to gossip concerning my actions and personal affairs, I hereby give notice that on and after this date I intend lying on my right side instead of my left as heretofore.

(Signed) "REUBEN WALL."

That this spirit should characterise an otherwise hospitable, amiable, and even cultured people, I ascribe in large part to a lack of opportunity on the part of the colonists to make themselves acquainted with what is happening from day to day in the great outside world. Will it be believed when I say that, although Newfoundland is a great centre or terminus of many Atlantic cables — that at Heart's Content thousands upon thousands of words and messages are passing and repassing on their way to London and Paris, New York and Chicago, Boston and Montreal — barely a word of this does the colonist see or hear. The deaf Cinderella holds the trumpet to her ear while speaks the wit and the commerce, the statesmanship and the art of two hemispheres, and wistfully wonders what it is all about. The world of civilisation palpitates with all that goes to make up our golden nineteenth-century heritage, and the genial current speeds to the Newfoundland shores; but by a whimsical fortune the cold rock alone feels its contact.

While enlightened public opinion is daily warming the heart and minds of 200,000,000 of people, the daily papers of St John's are busy calling each other "thieves" and "liars," "boodlers" and "sharks," and it is over this feeble flicker of recrimination that the inhabitants are expected to warm themselves.

The Governor of the Island, Sir Herbert Murray, K.C.B., is a widower. Anyone talking to him for five minutes must perceive that he has both great strength of character and executive ability, but that, as an Englishman who has spent his career at home in the Customs, he fatally misunderstands the colony, its needs, and, more emphatically, its politics.

Indeed, the Governors of Newfoundland continue to be, as they have been in the past, amiable gentlemen of advanced years, to whom the last idea that presents itself is a mingling with the politics of the island, a staunch support of their own Ministry, or a championship of the colony against the encroachments of the Foreign Office.

Newfoundland has the veriest shell of self-government: the kernel she never tasted.

CHAPTER V

Newfoundland is maligned as to fogs. Be that as it may, there is a fog, not a physical one — lowering, opaque, and impenetrable — a fog beside which the November blacknesses of London are but thin June mists. It has settled down over the island; it is called the French shore question.

To begin with, there exists a misapprehension as to the geographical situation of the fisheries themselves.

The French fisheries are two altogether distinct affairs. The one is the fishery on the Banks of Newfoundland, the other that which is undertaken on that portion of the Newfoundland coast commonly called the "French shore."

The fishing-grounds on the Banks lie along to the southward of the island, covering a great area, and distant from the coast of the colony about thirty miles at the nearest point. To these Banks—which are in effect huge submarine islands—the fishermen of France, Canada, America, and Newfoundland resort during the fishing season. These fishing-grounds are on the "high seas"; and therefore subject to the jurisdiction of no country or nation in particular. The Grand Banks are common property. With this fishery, therefore, the treaty business has no direct concern whatever. Its connection with Newfoundland is only in the fact that there exists on the south coast of Newfoundland a couple of islands called St Pierre and Miquelon, which form an entire and separate French colony, inhabited by an almost exclusively French population. From these islands the Bank fishing is prosecuted by the French in vessels, of which some come to St Pierre in the spring from France, and others are owned, kept, and fitted out in St Pierre. To these islands, for the purpose of curing and drying, the French fishermen bring the fish which they catch on the Banks. In the port of St Pierre, until recently, the French banking fleet have been accustomed to procure the greater part of their necessary supplies of bait, consisting of small fish taken by Newfoundland fishermen in the bays and harbours of Newfoundland adjacent to St Pierre. This bait is carried to the latter place by Newfoundland fishing craft, and sold to the French.

These two little French islands—the sole remnant of France's sovereignty in North America—are 140 miles distant from the nearest point of the so-called "French shore." The fishing-grounds to which the French fishermen resort on the Banks are about 100 miles from the same point, so that the reader will perceive that, geographically, as well as diplomatically, the French "rights" and "claims" on the Newfoundland coast have no real connection or relation whatever with the large and important business of the French fishery on the Banks, or with the French occupation or government of St Pierre and Miquelon. The Bank fishery, for which St Pierre is merely a basis of operations, is, as already stated, the common property of all nations, with which the treaties have nothing to do.

Yet, notwithstanding this, there has arisen latterly a very important connection—entirely unforeseen when the treaties were made—between the French claims on the "French shore" of Newfoundland and the Bank fishing from St Pierre.

But this is another branch of the muddle. It is as well to take one thing at a time.

The position of Newfoundland is unique among the colonies: although "daughter in her mother's house," she is by no means "mistress in her own." While the sovereignty of the entire territory is vested in Great Britain, a treaty with the French was made in 1713, under which their fishermen were granted fishing privileges along something more than half the coast of the colony. So far, so good. The island was unsettled. Nobody cared whether the French did or did not fish off the shore, or whether or not they occupied the shore afterwards for the purpose of drying their catch. But times changed. The treaty shore became by degrees settled by resident English fishermen; and for a century or so the English and the French pursued their vocation side by side. At last, the English settlers, discovering that the French were becoming more numerous than desirable, and believing that the island belonged to them as subjects of Great Britain, took occasion, when a British warship steamed alongside the shore, to appeal to its commander for protection. Wherever they laid their nets, they said, or established drying sheds, the French demolished them. The admiral looked over his instructions, landed his marines, who promptly took up more nets and tore down more sheds of the English! The native fishermen remonstrated.

"This land and these waters belong to us," they declared.

"Exactly," retorted the naval authorities; "for six months of the year—that is, from November to May—they are yours; but by the treaty of 1713 the French practically possess both for the remaining months."

"But that is precisely *our* fishing season!"

"The treaty explicitly says the French fishermen must not be interrupted. If your own fishing operations interrupt him, you must move on. This is the French interpretation of the treaty; and the British Government has, I regret to inform you, acquiesced in that interpretation. Our instructions are, in effect, 'Keep the peace between the French and the English. Protect the English if you can; go as far as possible in the assertion of their rights, but you must draw the line somewhere, and draw it at that point, wherever it may be, when danger of serious trouble with the French begins. And do not go beyond that limit, even though your holding back may involve hardship or injustice to the colonist; for if we are driven to choose between offending the French and neglecting to care for the colonist, the colonist must go to the wall.'"

This proceeding fell like a thunderbolt on the unfortunate colonists, the efforts of whose "village Hampdens" had at last, after a struggle of 150 years, succeeded in obtaining something like justice from the Mother Country, and in wresting from her reluctant parent the most elementary freedom and local government.

Those brave spirits, who throughout every hardship had striven to advance the island's prosperity, and to place it on the plane of its sister North American colonies, were chagrined and disheartened beyond measure.

For the line of coast comprehended by the

aforesaid treaty (or rather treaties, for there were four at different times between the two Governments) extends from Cape Ray, at the south-western extremity of the island, around the western, northern, and north-eastern shores to Cape St John, as will be seen by consulting the map. This territory is, in respect of soil, climate, forest, and mineral wealth, undoubtedly the most superior portion of Newfoundland. By these treaties it has been practically closed to settlement; and this fertile and promising West Coast, which would have been occupied by fishermen, farmers, lumbermen, and miners in great numbers, by factories, villages, and towns, is in this year of grace 1897 a region literally uninhabited.

Newfoundlanders are thus excluded from the fairer half of their own territory. Confined to the eastern and less desirable portion, they may, with the assurances of the English Government that all will yet be "satisfactorily adjusted," gaze longingly, like the Israelites, upon the Promised Land, an innocuous proceeding—one may reasonably hope still sanctioned by the French.

The Treaty of Utrecht, ratified in 1713, stipulates that the island of Newfoundland should belong of right wholly to Great Britain; that it shall be allowed to the subjects of France "to catch fish and dry them on land on that part only of the coast" defined in the treaty,

THE TENTH ISLAND

and that it shall not be lawful for the subjects of France to fortify any place in the said island, or to erect any buildings there besides stages made of boards and huts necessary and usual for drying of fish, or to resort to the said island beyond the time necessary for fishing and drying of fish.

Another treaty in 1783 provided that the French fishermen should not be "interrupted" in their labours by the English fishermen.

The next treaty dealing with the French on the subject of Newfoundland was that of Paris, 1763. Therein was renewed and confirmed the previous treaty, with the following article:— "The King of Great Britain cedes the islands of St Pierre and Miquelon in full right to His Most Christian Majesty, to serve as a shelter to French fishermen; and His Most Christian Majesty engages not to fortify the said islands, to erect no buildings upon them but merely for the convenience of the fishery, and to keep upon them a guard of fifty men only for the police."

En passant, it is significant to note that these conditions have been entirely disregarded by the French, who have made St Pierre a colony and erected defences and buildings of all kinds.

The Treaty of Versailles, 1783, was in confirmation of previous treaties, and in addition, a Declaration was attached to this treaty, by which His Britannic Majesty, "in order that the fishermen of the two nations might not give cause for daily quarrels," engaged to "take the most positive measures for preventing his subjects from interrupting in any manner by their competition the fishery of the French during the temporary exercise of it which is granted to them upon the coast of the island of Newfoundland; but he will for this purpose cause the fixed settlements which shall be formed there to be removed."

This was quite in keeping with England's traditional throttling policy towards her firstborn colony.

The Treaty of Paris, 1815, confirmed the previous arrangements, and no modification or alteration has since been made.

So long as the French shore remained unsettled it was really not worth while for the Quai d'Orsay to bother its head about the matter. France sent her fishermen to the Grand Banks, away to the south-east of Newfoundland, where the fishery was infinitely more profitable. Indeed, had the treaty shore become settled without some discordant agency, some fermenting spirit, we should have heard little or nothing of the terrible French shore question.

But as the coast became dotted with villages an old controversy as to whether the French fishing privileges were concurrent or exclusive was revived. Nobody could see exactly why it was revived; the sovereignty of the island seemed securely vested with the British; the French had nothing to gain by coming so far for their fish when they were debarred from settling on the territory, or even permitted to remain after a certain date each year.

The British might have revived, too, the theory that when the adjoining islands of St Pierre and Miquelon were ceded to the French in 1763, it was under a distinct agreement that they should not fortify the place or station troops there, that no foreign ship should enter the port, and that an English commissary should be allowed to reside in St Pierre. All four conditions have been violated: therefore the islands revert to the British.

To support this revival of a doubtful interpretation, to say the least, the disputed shore must be fortified by greater numbers of French fishermen. But the shrewd, sturdy tribes from Brittany and the Basque Provinces could not be tempted to leave the Banks for the Treaty shore, even for the prospect of rubbing shoulders with the Englishmen. The opportunity was not one to be lost, and a bounty, therefore, amounting to a third of the market price of the fish, was ordered to be paid to the French fishermen. This bounty annually amounts to many thousands of pounds. The French

Government pays it cheerfully. Its fishermen, armed by this bounty, are enabled to make Treaty shore-fishing profitable.

That was only the beginning. The Quai d'Orsay determined to push matters to a conclusion. They declared that, their rights being exclusive, it would no longer be possible for the colonist to fish at all in his own waters. This was bad enough, but the Note went on to say that the shore itself was theirs as well. A railway had just been projected—the survey was completed — the first sod cut. Downing Street was appealed to — the terminus would be in French territory. The British Liberal Government ordered the railway to be abandoned.

One reason advanced by the French I must not omit to record. It was delivered, besides, with great gravity.

The screeching of the railway locomotive would frighten away the fish.

Thenceforward no mills, no piers, no structures of any kind were countenanced by the French, and the Newfoundlanders woke up one fine morning to find themselves called "foreigners" by M. Waddington, in his Note to Lord Rosebery, the Foreign Minister. The Ford-Pennell convention was held, but fizzled out without coming to terms on the question of exclusive or concurrent rights. The situation then remained as before. Great Britain and France pounded away at each other, and Newfoundland got all the blows. This, also, as before.

Driven in desperation to do something, the unfortunate colonists hit upon the catching and canning of lobsters. Here was a profitable industry, and one from which, by the very nature of the process, the French were debarred. Lobsters may or may not be classed as fish to-day, but they were clearly not in the mind of the negotiators of these antiquated treaties. Moreover, how could the treaty privilege of "drying" be construed into "canning"? Such factories must be permanent buildings—with bricked boilers and corrugated iron roofs. By 1889 they were flourishing—sixty of these lobster factories. To their confusion, the French followed suit in the industry. Lobster catching and canning they defined as fishing and drying, and the unscrupulous French agents clamoured for the removal of the British factories. The British admiral again came gallantly to the rescue of the French. But the work of demolishing the factories was suddenly interrupted.

A strange and startling discovery was made: to wit, that the Act of Parliament empowering British naval officers to enforce these treaties had expired by virtue of its own provisions in the year 1834 and had never been renewed. Wherefore, from that time forward, no legal authority had existed for the enforcement of the British Government's instructions to naval commanders upon the coast of Newfoundland.

Downing Street, informed that these illegal enforcements had been going on for fifty-six years, was taken completely by surprise. Sir Baldwin Walker, the gallant British admiral, was sued in the courts, and mulcted in 5000 dollars, and at length, after much ado, an objectionable *modus vivendi* was agreed upon. While it continues, no more lobster factories can be erected, and the colony has to put up with the loss of £40,000 a year.

I spoke of a sinister agency at work somewhere throughout the whole later French shore treaty business. I now purpose disclosing what —or more properly, who—that agency is.

CHAPTER VI

AND what is this sinister agency—this "worm i' the bud" of Newfoundland's progress.

In the light of my further inquiries into the vexed French shore question of to-day, it contracts—the units become proportionate—its perplexities fade away or fall into their proper places—the theme is shot with colour—and lo! what was a Blue-book becomes a romance. What follows might be a chapter from Sue or Stevenson; it is actual fact.

In a two-storey wooden house in St John's I have discovered the greatest diplomatist on earth. I take some pride in the quality of my discovery. France has had many clever spies and persuasive emissaries; but she has, I make bold to say, none more clever or persuasive than Monsieur C. Riballier des Isles.

It should be understood that M. des Isles has been a great patriot all his life. From his entry into the Consular service, many years ago, he varied his official duties by reading the history of his nation, its conquests, and its defeats.

Its conquests stirred his soul; its defeats pained and humiliated him.

In the course of time M. des Isles was sent to

Quebec—that once proud capital of the French North American dominions—and it was here that, marrying a lady of pronounced Anglophobe tendencies, a splendid scheme sprang into his brain. He declared he could no longer remain in Canada while it was under the British flag, and forthwith got himself transferred to the little French colony of St Pierre, off the Newfoundland coast. Up to that moment the French shore question had practically no diplomatic value. Let us be concise: Monsieur C. Riballier des Isles *is* the French shore question.

This humble little gentleman, peacefully strolling the St John's streets, and invariably shown the outside of every official door, is the author of the whole wretched business.

In 1883-4 all French diplomatic circles—nay, every man, woman, and child in France and her colonies—understood that "all the rights of France in Newfoundland were definitely and finally surrendered and completely extinguished" by the Treaty of Utrecht in 1713. M. Gambetta had admitted it. M. de Freycinet admitted it. It was left for one lonely little Consul in St Pierre to make the startling assertion that a good half of Newfoundland—our oldest colony—belonged to France. He returned home and laid the case before his superior officer. A week afterwards he was informed that M. de Freycinet had considered

THE TENTH ISLAND

it "untenable." The Consul was politely ordered back to the post he had quitted.

Then something happened to change the mind of the Government with regard to the scheme. It was laid before the Cabinet. The Cabinet were delighted. M. des Isles was sent out as a Consul to —— Newfoundland. Anything to make trouble with the British Government—anything to divert attention from certain manœuvres of France elsewhere. His instructions were the vaguest imaginable, and amounted in effect to this: "We know nothing of this question. Make your own case, and, right or wrong, we will back you up."

M. des Isles then went to Newfoundland—not in any official capacity—because the Newfoundlanders refused to receive him—but as a French spy. Lest I be thought injudicious, I will state the exact language of Judge Prowse to me:— "The status of M. des Isles in this colony is that of a French spy."

For eleven years this energetic little gentleman has laboured to bring about unpleasantness between England and France. At one time it looked like war; had Newfoundland been in greater proximity to the Mother Country it would have been war. He has incited the colonists almost to rebellion against Great Britain, and has cost their Treasury and their merchants millions of dollars. He has personally stirred up inoffensive French fishermen to take advantage of "rights" which are impossible under the several treaties, and, in short, I have made only a plain statement of fact when I said that but for the existence of Riballier des Isles, the French shore question would not cause another diplomatic pang.

M. des Isles is the avowed author of the following remarkable *dictum*, which was laid before Lord Salisbury by the French Ambassador in 1890:—"France preserved the exclusive right of fishing she always had. The right of France to the coast of Newfoundland reserved to her fishermen is only a part of her ancient sovereignty over the island which she retained in ceding the soil to England, and which she has never weakened or alienated."

If M. des Isles was indefatigable before, thenceforward he became colossal. He travelled incessantly on the treaty coast. He talked with the fishing compatriots—he explained to them the situation, and urged them to assume the "dog-in-the-manger policy" upon every opportunity. The British Government shuffled with its responsibility, and at length, by the fatal *modus vivendi*, agreed to disagree with the French Government.

This was an evil move : for it gave some shadow of right to the French contention. A *modus vivendi* in such circumstances is but the feeble trick of a destitute statesmanship.

The Consul had asked for French warships to take up the nets and tear down the sheds of the English. On hearing, however, of the *modus vivendi*, he countermanded the request. The British warships would now perform the agreeable task. They did it, sorrowfully and reluctantly; but they did it, as I have already explained. They are doing it to-day. The objectionable *modus vivendi* continues; it is renewed from time to time; the impudent contention of the French grows with precedent. Last year, I am told, a Frenchman landed at the Bay of Islands. "Bay des Isles," he cried, raising his hat in the air. "At last—at last we have regained our own!"

In England we should call Riballier a mischief-maker and a spy. In France the Government has just loaded him with decorations—he is an officer, and will soon be a commander in the Legion of Honour, and he has just been created Consul-General to Newfoundland.

In person it is difficult to withold admiration from M. des Isles. He is a typical French detective—thin, yellow, and with the eyes of a ferret. His English is execrable; nothing escapes him—he is continually on the watch, and he strives to ingratiate himself with everybody. I approached him cautiously.

"Will any solution be achieved of the French shore question?" I asked.

"There is no question," sententiously replied the quasi-Consul.

"Then France is in the right?"

"*Parfaitement!* There is the treaty."

"But which treaty?"

"One will suffice. The *modus vivendi* will exist for centuries."

"But suppose we abrogate the treaty?"

The Consul smiled cynically, shrugging his shoulders.

"You dare not. The business of your Government at present is to fulfil its obligations. But if you like, tear up the treaty, and put us out—if you can."

"But will France not listen to terms? Will she not make a settlement on the basis of exchange in return for St Pierre and the treaty rights? There is Dominica, for example."

"Never. It is a matter of sentiment. This is the sole relic (with St Pierre) of our North American dominions. The case is this: You English have possession here of a house, and you have given us the right to occupy the parlour. We take you at your word. We are comfortable, and we intend to remain. But, sapristi! you English say, 'We do not like you there. You make too much noise. You hammer against the wall; you destroy the furniture.' 'Never mind,' we say, 'it is ours to destroy. We are comfortable.' *J'y suis, j'y reste.* No, you are

THE TENTH ISLAND

wise. Newfoundland is only one of your colonies. You cannot afford to be rash for her sake. No, Monsieur, you have your Empire to look after."

"But," I ventured to observe, "the treaty coast will be built up, the French will be forced to retire."

"We will see to that," responded Riballier; and then he added, "I do not know what the Newfoundland Government can have been about, that it has not made a milch cow of the British Government on account of this question. But they are foolish; they have not got a *sou*."

On the whole treaty shore the French have 987 men employed in cod-fishing, and the total number of their fishing vessels on the coast is twenty-seven. In the lobster fishery they have 200 men, and the value of their catch last season was about £30,000.

To obtain this insignificant sum they occupy a coast line of over 500 miles, and though they have only certain concurrent fishing rights, they press these so pertinaciously and aggressively that they have actually succeeded in occupying the best half of the island, and prevented hitherto the development of its rich natural resources. By the treaty they have no territorial rights whatever, but in maintaining their fishing rights they keep up an incessant worry and uneasiness, and frequently endanger the

E

peace of two great nations. To France the treaty shore represents a loss, but whatever their nature they refuse to be bought out or to exchange it for territory elsewhere.

One of the delegates to England in 1890, Mr Scott, Q.C., made the following statement to me:—"It is the clear and settled conviction of the whole people of the colony," said Mr Scott—"the result of law and better experience, and of a full knowledge of the whole subject—that upon no other basis than that of an entire extinguishment (of course upon some honourable and satisfactory terms) of French rights and pretensions in the colony of Newfoundland can there be any solution of the difficulties which have now become so grave and acute. To no settlement of the French shore question which does not contain this as an essential basis will the colonists agree."

England and her Ministers have persistently refused to acknowledge that the treaties conveyed any exclusive right to the French; but what is a refusal that is not carried to the moral length of an ultimatum? When in 1886 France, fortified by England's evidently moderate attitude, again put forward its claims to exclusive rights, threatening to confiscate the gear of any that were found fishing on that coast, to disregard the jurisdiction of the colonial magistrates, to prevent the working of mines, and to forcibly protect French fishermen in taking salmon and lobsters as well as cod, Lord Rosebery, then Foreign Minister, responded as follows:—

"I have no desire to re-open the discussion on the numerous points in dispute; but I cannot refrain from deprecating more particularly the claim put forward by your Government to ignore during the fishing season the territorial jurisdiction flowing from the sovereign rights of the British Crown over the whole of the island of Newfoundland, expressly conferred by the thirteenth article of the Treaty of Utrecht; nor can I pass in silence the reiterated assertion in your note of an exclusive right of fishing on the part of the coast on which the French treaty rights exist. There can be no doubt that the inhabitants must not 'interrupt by their competition the French fishermen'; but Her Majesty's Government can hardly believe that the French Government could intend to apply to them the term 'foreigner'; or to question the right of the colonists to procure the means of subsistence by fishing on their own coasts, so long as they do not interfere with the treaty rights of the French fishermen. Such a claim has no precedent in history; and would be not only repugnant to reason, but opposed to the practice of trade and to the actual terms of the Declaration of Versailles,* which provide that the old methods of fishing 'shall not be deviated from by either party,' showing conclusively that the French right to the fishery is not an exclusive one."

In 1889, when the lobster-canning episode to which I have alluded arose, the colonists believed that the whole wretched business had been brought to a head. Surely the Imperial Government's apathy was now at an end. Burning with zealous indignation, they despatched a delegation to England to lay their grievances before Parliament and the British nation. The Government seemed to lend a sympathetic ear; and the English press lent its outspoken support. The delegates returned to Newfoundland; and the Government began a series of remonstrances with France, who obstinately refused to budge an inch from their position. Wearied by their pertinacity, the British Government offered to submit the lobster question to arbitration.

Herein the Mother Country reckoned without

---

*The French knew well how weak their case is on the treaties, so in all their official correspondence they fall back on the Declaration of George III. in 1783 attached to the Treaty of Versailles. I have shown under what fraudulent circumstances that treaty was made. It was part of a treaty. Now it is a well-recognised principle that a treaty and all its concomitants is abrogated by war. To make that declaration legal and binding upon the English Government, it should have been repeated in succeeding treaties, but it was never renewed.—D. W. PROWSE.

her colony—to whom she had given a solemn undertaking, under date of March 26, 1857,* to consummate no affairs relating to itself without the previous knowledge and sanction of its Legislature. For the French accepted arbitration; and without consulting Newfoundland, the Imperial Government arranged with the French the before-mentioned *modus vivendi*. The resentment of the unfortunate colony knew no bounds. The Legislature, which opened March 6th, 1890, unanimously adopted resolutions condemning the *modus vivendi*; and mass meetings of the people denounced it in the strongest language. But Newfoundland's protest came too late: England had pledged herself to France; and the arrangement went into operation to the colony's detriment, and in spite of its indignation.

In the language of M. des Isles: Newfoundland is only one of our colonies; we cannot afford to be rash for her sake. We cannot even afford to be just and honest for her sake. We have much more important work to look after elsewhere.

A *modus vivendi* cannot, however, endure for ever: especially when it is continued without the colony's moral consent. Nor can any intelligent person, on reviewing the case I have here but crudely presented, believe that any of the French pretensions to the island can endure.

---

* *The Tenth Islanders call this document their Magna Charta. The signature appended to it is " Henry Labouchere."*

CHAPTER VII

WHATEVER may be the future of Newfoundland, she has had a past in the cod-fish.

Amidst the direst pangs she has suffered of contumely and neglect, one friend—and one friend alone—has remained at her side, or, more properly speaking, at her coasts, with almost touching constancy. And now, they say, the cod-fish is leaving her.

The cod fisheries of Newfoundland are still the greatest in the world; but they appertain, as I have shown, chiefly to the Grand Banks. Newfoundland itself has long supplied Spain, Portugal, Italy, and Brazil with that most substantial and palatable product of the sea.

Newfoundland has even her commercial traditions.

There used to be, in the '40's and '50's, a deferential duty in favour of Spain, amounting to four shillings a quintal. For several years there were often sixty and seventy Spanish vessels loading fish in the port of St John's alone, and a large number at Harbour Grace. Many of these were slavers: you could see the ring-bolts in the hold, to which the wretched Africans were chained. Spanish onzos and

THE TENTH ISLAND 71

Mexican dollars were then common, even to abundance, in the island. But the alteration in the tariff, doing away with the preference given to Spain, ended this trade.

When I had spent a week or so in the capital, I turned to the nearest outport where I could behold the "noble cod," as the Newfoundland writers term him, if not in all his glory, at least in all his degradation.

A chaste Yankee writer observed that, of all animals, a dried cod-fish appeared to him the most "helpless and homely."

Certainly the noble cod's relations would have difficulty in identifying him when the art of the fish-maker has put in its broader touches.

As was to be expected, one hears a great deal of fish and fish-making outside St John's, where, indeed, the subject is slightly tabooed for its vulgarity; and to a stranger ear "fish-making" has a whimsical sound. But the fish-maker is a simple, not too skilful person, usually the wife, son, or daughter of the fisherman. The fisherman himself, pleased with his exploits and the extent of his catch, surveys their performances from the adjacent cottage—fortified by his bottle and pipe.

There are a number of little square one-storey cottages jumbled together at the bottom of a high hill, looking very much as if they had rolled down from that eminence and not since been straightened out, or even put right side up. In the vicinity of each is a strip of herbage, upon which a goat browses; while from an open window comes the robust squalling of an infant, and the pungent perfume of an odoriferous stew.

Such is Quidi Vidi, a typical fishing village.

Out into the water of the little harbour or inlet, which laps the rocky beach, are erected the stages at which the men land their fish, and where the scaled creatures are received by each of their families or helpers and subjected to the necessary processes of "splitting," "heading," and "salting." This accomplished, the decapitated cloven fish are dragged in their thousands to the "flakes"—rude scaffolds, covered with under-brush—and there spread out to dry.

The surroundings are not unpicturesque. Fantastic brown cliffs almost completely environ the spot. The little fishing-boats dance and caper in the green waters. A tiny white cascade tumbles over the rocks into the harbour. An aged dame in a red shawl sits at the door of one of the cottages knitting. The arm of her son, a great burly fisherman, is on her shoulder. A glass of rum is in his hand (he has just offered me a similar glass, which I have lamely declined), and he is even more in the mood for talking than usual.

"There'll be seventy quintals there," he says

complacently; "allowing fifty fish to the quintal: and that'll make two hundred and ten dollars coming to me. But last season was a bad one, and I owe a hundred and fifty dollars to the 'planter'—so that I'll have a bare sixty dollars over and above. But ye'll have your new shawl, mother; an' Katie yonder'll have her calico; an' I'll borrow a bit against the sealing time."

And so these tough, sturdy fellows live on, apparently from hand to mouth — unlettered themselves, knowing no horizon that is not bounded by a cod-fish wall, nor any pleasures that are not of the rudest and most primitive order. But their sons and daughters, during the winter time, are being taken in hand by the priest, clergyman, or minister, and taught to read and write, and derive from chance books and papers an idea of that vast intellectual turmoil that is going on thousands of miles away. The Newfoundland fisherman inhabiting a hundred such villages is, in sooth, a burly, uncouth personage, whose salvation lies in his brawn: for while he has been storing up physical energy, the rest of mankind has been wasting it; and that sinew and energy, unless I am much mistaken, will stand him or his descendants in very good stead when Newfoundland's time comes.

Although the returns for the last ten years

show, perhaps, a slight decrease in the amount of the annual catch, yet the authorities are slow to believe that the cod-fisheries are declining. Only each year it is plain the fisherman is obliged to move farther afield for his fish. Once he could cast a line or net in his own bays and harbours within sight of his own cot, and drag up the cod by the hundreds. Now he must sail out to the Banks with the rest, or along to Labrador—worse luck!

The reason for the vast sea harvest which has for centuries centred about this island is most interesting. It seems that the Arctic current which flows past Newfoundland carries with it a vast slime—hundreds of thousands of tons of minute living matter, upon which the small crustaceans, annelids, and mollusca feed. In turn, these latter become the aliment of the vast schools of cod which are lying in wait for it there. It is strange, but true, that the Arctic seas and rivers, in spite of the great cold with which they are surrounded, contribute most abundantly to this supply of living slime. Unless something like a convulsion of nature occurs, and this flood from the Pole is arrested, the fishermen cannot with every ordinary resource at their command cause any perceptible diminution in the general supply of cod.

Its annual average for eighty years has been about the same.

THE TENTH ISLAND

Yet the apparatus for taking fish is greatly increased, besides being more efficient in every way, and there are thrice as many persons engaged in the industry as there were early in the century. Cod-traps, huge seines, nets, bultows, jiggers, are some of the implements introduced in recent times; and the primitive hook and line of earlier times is used by a comparatively small number of fishermen. In the opinion of some of the natives, this stationary condition of the fishery, when one considers the new Labrador fields now at the disposal of the fishermen, is due to the "reckless and destructive modes of fishing, unrestrained by any legal enactments, or proper rules and regulations," which have been practised for generations. Whether this view be just or not, there certainly could not have been any harm in placing the whole fishery of the island, as was done recently, upon a scientific basis. The destruction of young fish before reaching a reproductive age should certainly be prohibited; and the observance of "close seasons," when the fish are spawning, insisted upon.

At present the demand for dried cod-fish does not seem destined to fall off. It could be considerably stimulated if there was any systematic effort made to introduce it into countries like Africa, or if the conditions of the industry were characterised by that enterprise and ability which marks other trades. But even if the universal consumption were increased, as I shall proceed to show, it would, under the economic conditions at present prevailing abroad, scarcely benefit Newfoundland.

The total value of the exports from the colony amount to something under 6,660,691 dollars annually. The number of those engaged in the fishery is about 55,000. The salmon, herring, and lobster fisheries are also carried on on the shores and bays of the island. The number of men engaged in the lobster factories is about 3400, and 1400 women.

Norway, Newfoundland's nearest rival, exports annually 50,000,000 cod-fish. The aggregate annual catch of cod in these waters by French, American, Canadian, and Newfoundland fishermen is estimated at 3,700,000 quintals. Allowing fifty fish to a quintal, the total number of cod would be 185,000,000. As "every bullet has its billet," so every one of this enormous number of cod-fish finds a stomach — and finding it empty, fills it.

There is nothing so filling as cod-fish.

The Roman Catholic countries alone spend a million pounds sterling annually in the purchase of Newfoundland and Canadian cod-fish. If they turned Protestant to-morrow, and Lent and Friday fasts were abolished—Newfoundland would then be forced to find other markets for her staple product, or else to adopt a different method in handling and exporting it.

Dried cod would then be found to have had its day; and the era of fresh fish, which is the source of such vast wealth to Europe, would perforce begin. The product of the North Sea fisheries is worth sixteen millions sterling annually, the value of British fish alone being eight million pounds; yet strange to relate, apart from the oyster fishery, the whole deep-sea fisheries of America are well under three millions. England, with half the population, consumes three times as much fish as America. It is not that the American palate does not naturally relish a fish diet, but the facilities for carriage inland are so imperfect, and the price generally so high, that it has never become a food staple in anything approaching the same measure that it has in England. Judge Prowse of St John's has long been a believer in the establishment of a market for fresh cod in the American cities. "The old-fashioned plan of salting and drying the codfish must be abandoned," he says; "it is most absurd and wasteful to actually destroy two-thirds of a most valuable article of food in order to render the remainder uneatable. What we require is a new method of selling our fish in its most palatable form fresh."

There certainly seems a great future for Newfoundland cod, salmon, and lobsters—if one considers the now increased facilities for transportation afforded by the new railway, and the price which these articles fetch in the island as compared with the ordinary quotations in fish-markets of New York. Salmon of a superior quality is valued at only five cents (2½d.) and lobsters fivepence a dozen. In New York salmon is from forty to fifty cents a pound, and lobsters from thirty-five to seventy-five cents apiece. We have only to compare these prices with those obtained in England—to contrast the plenteousness of lobster, salmon, and trout with which the rivers, lakes, and bays of Newfoundland teem, in order to appreciate the opportunities which lie within the reach of the Tenth Island to secure a place for its products even in Billingsgate Fish Market. Transportation, if undertaken under favourable circumstances, is only a matter of three or four days; and when mutton is carried fourteen thousand miles, and fresh cod, mackerel, and oysters into Texas and Colorado—the capabilities of the cold storage system are instantly perceived.

Even as matters stand, the Newfoundlanders assure us that their cod-fish has not really declined in value in communities where it is not brought into unfair competition with the bounty-fed product. On the contrary, it has advanced more than fifty per cent. within the last twenty-five years. Under new and improved methods of cure and packing, in such communities it finds a readier market, and its flavour is declared finer than the Norwegian article. One might have travelled yesterday in Spain or Portugal and, in the most remote and primitive villages, have been regaled with a dish made from the prized *baccalhao* or *curadillo*, as is still called from the Basques that which once swam innocently in Newfoundland waters, and was "split," "headed," "salted," and "dried" by Newfoundland swains and maidens.

To-day it is all—or nearly all—French " bounty fish."

The article known as "boneless cod-fish" is increasing in popularity: the manufacture of cod-liver oil is profitable; the best glue is made from the skin of the cod, and a much-prized fertiliser is obtained from the bones and head. In short, every portion of the cod-fish can be put to a good and profitable use. To go through one of the great fishing establishments of St John's or the outports, is of itself a speedy education in the value and uses of the cod-fish.

It is a pity the cod has not more picturesque personality. I could find it easier to write about him with enthusiasm.

A sad neglect has overtaken the Newfoundland herring fishery. Otherwise the herring might have proved as profitable as it formerly did to the Dutch, whose city of Amsterdam had a "foundation of herring bones." Herring is employed chiefly for bait; but they are to be had in inexhaustible quantities, and some £35,000 sterling worth is annually exported. The trouble with the herring industry is that the Newfoundlanders never took the pains in curing and packing that they should have done. Their product, therefore, has managed to obtain a reputation for inferiority, which an improved method is doing its best to put down.

The canning of lobsters was a great success from the start; and I believe the men engaged on the west coast in this industry are making money, and plenty of it. About two million one-pound tins were exported last year.

In the old days the Newfoundlander stuck to his plain, dried cod with a blind devotion —neither viewing nor seeking anything further to enhance his fortunes. Even cod-glue and cod-fertiliser left him cold, and cod-liver oil stirred him to no more enthusiasm than it stirs in the nursery. Now he is just waking up from that lazy contempt which he felt for the herring, salmon, and lobster innovators: and the day may even come when he will merely hand over his catch of cod fresh to the merchant, and allow his wife and family, released from arduous "salting" and "drying," to devote themselves to his and their moral and more æsthetic welfare in the kitchen and garden.

CHAPTER VIII

THOMAS CODLIN is a "planter" of one of the outports. The title of his profession takes us back to the time when all the colonies were plantations and the colonists "planters." In person, Codlin is above the middle height, tan-visaged, and burly. He is not too particular about his dress, which is patched and weather-beaten, and he wears a beard à la *Terre-Neuve*—*i.e.* unkempt and straggling. Mr Codlin is a capitalist on a small scale, and having through his clientèle some political influence, he has developed a taste for politics. As a matter of fact, Mr Codlin is the "middleman" between the fisherman and the merchant. He takes his supplies—groceries, dry-goods, and fishing requisites—from the merchant in St John's, with whom he has a standing account, and doles out such supplies from time to time in advance to the fishermen. For the fisherman as a rule lives a hand-to-mouth existence; and the product of a fair season, instead of enriching him, only leaves him just quits with our friend the planter. But this is not Mr Codlin's fault; indeed, he is for ever declaring it to be his misfortune.

"Rich, Jim Bate? Come, man, don't talk like a fool. How d'ye s'pose I'm going to make money with such seasons as the last two, an' the price o' fish what it is? I've got mor'n twenty bad debts on my books, and who d' ye s'pose supports Houligan and Briggs, what have been laid up these eighteen months? If the boys bring in the fish, I'll pay the money every time and willingly; but if they don't bring it in, well, we're both in a hole, that's all."

"Sure," says a man in the fishing-room, pulling hard tack out of his pocket, "it's all very weel, Mr Codlin, but is it no true ye're after sending your son and daughter home to England for their education?"

"Ay, ay," cry the others, who, though tall and big-boned, have undeniably a hungry look; "is that a fact, sor?"

The "planter" turns almost fiercely on his interlocutors.

"True! Mike Shea, ye'd believe every lie ye heard about me? No, it's not true, and even if it were, I should like to know who'd a better right to do as he pleases with the precious little money he could ever make here. I've stuck to this outport for twenty years. I was one of you, boys, and a sealer myself, until my grandfather left me the seven hundred dollars he had saved. I've stuck here twenty years; and cursed sorry I am, too, for with the same capital and half the work, I reckon I could ha' sent my gal to St John's for the winter 'thout being bullied for it. You, Michael Shea, I've given you supplies when no other planter in Harbour Grace 'd ha' trusted you wi' so much as a dozen o' hooks; an' I've taken risks with ye all without weel seein' me way clear, an' more than once been on the verge o' bankruptcy for me pains. An' what ha' ye done for me, faith? Three years gone, when I stood for the Legislature, ye all came nobly forward and voted against me to a man."

"Sure ye're wrong there," spoke up several voices. "I give ye my vote." "An' so did I." "And I too, Mr Codlin."

"So all I can say is," went on Mr Codlin without heeding the interruptions, "if ye can get along better without me, ye're welcome to try. See if Simpson and Grant, or ould Munro give ye better terms."

Whereupon the indignant planter began stalking up and down the great piles of cod outside the fishing-house, on the wharf, stopping here and there to take a brown carcase and smack it viciously against the others; or give orders to the two or three men who were engaged in loading the fish on the schooner for St John's.

The price of fish is regulated by the demand for it in foreign markets and by the quantity taken. The larger the catch in the island and in Norway, the island's greatest rival, the lower the price. But from talks I have had with the planters, the greatest possible alarm is felt at the continuous loss of markets which once belonged to Newfoundland as of right. The cause of this will be seen when I come to speak of the action of the French bounty system. It seems that the operation of the French bounties has so lowered the price of fish in the markets of Europe as to make the fishing far less profitable to the colonists than formerly. Fish now brings about 14s. a quintal (112 lbs.) In recent days the sale price was anywhere from 15s. to 20s., even going as high as 25s. on occasion. Naturally the price of fish is a great topic in the outports—just as the price of wheat is of mighty importance to the farmer. Peter Anderson, who caught 120 quintals the past season, is elated beyond measure —until he discovers that Codlin, owing to the quality of the fish and the lowness of the market price, can only afford to credit him with 12s. a quintal, and he owes that amiable gentleman for provisions £72, 15s.—which balance of 15s. the planter generously offers to overlook.*

The fisherman's great grievance is that he is absolutely at the mercy of such petty capitalists as Thomas Codlin. If he has only a moderate quantity of fish to turn over each season—what with the high prices charged for provisions by his "planter," he can never quite reach a balance in his favour—and a single bad season throws

---

* *It is said that seventeen tons of fish contain the nutritive value of 50 head of cattle or 300 sheep. The average annual yield from the fisheries is 2,300,000 cwts.*—i.e. 338,235 *cattle or* 2,029,410 *sheep.*

him "all out of gear" for years afterwards. I heard of a hard-working fellow, with a large family, who had been twenty-three years in debt to his "planter." Each season he would try harder than ever to extricate himself, but without success. He had got apparently hopelessly into the power of Codlin, who used him pretty much as an English farmer of the old school might be supposed to use a tenant long in arrears. Such complete thraldom would have broken the spirit of most men, and that is pretty nearly the way it acted on this old fellow. Once or twice, it is true, he landed as much as 90 quintals in a single season; but the whole lot went into the capacious hand of the middleman; and still the balance was against him. And then it was that he took to drink, losing all hope, and his family turned against him and treated him in a heartless manner, as being the cause of all their misfortunes. His two sons were rather sickly, and therefore not able to make any very strong bid for fortune. Once they came upon their father dead drunk, with liquor whose cost put him still farther into debt and the clutches of the planter, and they left him where he lay. The next morning he was found by a neighbour nearly perished with cold.

One March day this man was missing. The truth was he had tramped across country to a neighbouring outport where he was unknown, and by luck, at the last moment, got a berth on a big sealer where a fever had broken out. In less than a month that sealer was back in port with one of the biggest cargoes ever landed—some 40,000 harp seals. The old man's share, under the peculiar circumstances, was about three hundred dollars. He returned to his native outport, paid the planter; and the next day his dead body was found swinging to one of the rafters of the latter's fish-house. He had committed suicide, either because the wiped-off debt had turned his brain, or because he thought it best to avoid further unpleasantness.

But, of course, this all illustrates only one side of the story. Codlin's statement of the case of the planter is capital's defence all the world over. Either the merchant or the middleman has to take the risks of the business as well as the fisherman, and there is little doubt that in bad seasons his loss is considerable. Somebody has got to keep the poor fisherman going—to tide him over—and the Banks and large merchants do not show much disposition to treat with this class. To mortgage the prospective cod harvest is not quite so safe as mortgaging a prospective wheat crop. It is all very well for a certain class in the colony to rail at the middleman and the credit system, but it is a little difficult to see how either are to be dispensed with. The system began when the island was settled; it has gone on for so many generations that it is for the most part accepted by the fishermen themselves as a necessary institution; and if they dearly love to rail at the planter, it is only because of the natural modern attitude of the man who has no money towards the man who has.

Life in the fishing villages is very near to the earth—or rather to the sea. It is hard to remember you are not in a forecastle when you visit the cottages or meeting-places of the inhabitants. The populace is almost entirely composed of fishermen—the exceptions being the merchants or planters, a few tradesmen, the priest, the clergyman, and the doctor. The daily round of the masses, when not varied by agricultural pursuits, is unattractive and sordid to a degree. In the winter there is deer-shooting for the few, but the majority of the men do little besides mend their nets and fishing-tackle, smoke, drink, spin yarns, and wait for the March sealing season to commence. The women do most of the work. I have seen them chopping wood and digging with a spade, while their lords, pipe in mouth, looked approvingly on, slowly recovering from the more or less arduous labour of two months previously.

But some of them go in for farming, and the number of these is greatly on the increase. If they were wise they would all alternate the two employments, certainly on a sufficiently large scale to guarantee them potatoes, a cow, and a pig. An annual agricultural fair is now held in St John's, and the display will certainly compare favourably with similar shows held in any place of equal size on the continent. It gives the fisherman-farmer a chance to exhibit his produce to advantage, and to promote a healthy emulation between all of his class.

I do not say the fisherman's life is not picturesque. Life in the forecastle is undeniably picturesque. But there is a sense of being shut in—of the narrowness of life's possibilities and opportunities—that must weigh heavily on the young soul that was not born a sailor or a sealer. There are still two solid diversions for the Newfoundlander of the outports — getting drunk and attending meetings. He has such happy dispensations as weddings and funerals; but these are of minor import.

Then there is that old west-country pastime known as "mummers." Mummers, I should conceive, was in existence long before the miracle play; for a mere rudimentary dramatic form is absolutely impossible. The first thing for the organiser to do is to choose a theme — say, "Jack of the Beanstalk" or "Joan of Arc"—allot to each person his or her "part," and leave the rest to chance. Chance forthwith ordains that whichever "mummer" comes on to the stage or circle attired in the most extravagant and outlandish garb is at once the prime favourite. If he can improve the occasion with some impromptu jokes and sallies, so much the better.

"Mummers" smacks of the nursery—of the nursery at that period when children *romped* instead of dissecting Norwegian plays and reading more-or-less improving books as they, alas, do now; but given the requisite number of spirited young swains and rosy-cheeked girls, and I am quite ready to back "mediæval mummers" against even a modern musical comedy.

The physician in charge of the lunatic asylum told me that religious excitement was at the bottom of much of the lunacy of the colony. Another prominent cause was too close intermarriage. It would do no harm if the tables of consanguinity were impressed upon the more remotely-situated communities by Government.

As to the character of the meetings which are the fisherman's weakness, that, I opine, is largely a question of race. If he comes most of English or Scottish extraction, a good revival gathering of the Baptist or Salvation Army order will most touch the heart of himself and his women-folk; if he be Milesian, there is a strain in his blood which is ever mounting towards a caucus. Occasionally he is gratified by a riot; but these are growing fewer and fewer nowadays. Denominational feeling runs less high than it used to, and it is now many years since the feuds of Orangemen and the Roman Catholics caused public bloodshed. The last great riots took place in connection with the new railway, of which I shall speak when I come to that part of my subject; but they illustrate clearly the great ignorance and fanaticism of the fishermen. If another illustration were wanted, I hardly think a better one could be found than in the superstitious antagonism to confederation with Canada. There are thousands of fishermen and the wives of fishermen on the southern and north-eastern coasts who believe to-day that Canada is a land of demons and monsters, just as the more ignorant Southerners of the States during the Civil War believed the Yankees had horns and tails. The most singular legends exist in the bosom of these humble families. They have heard that "new-born babes are rammed down Canadian cannon," that if confederation was brought about, the terrible Canadians would usurp their industries, leaving them to "bleach their bones on the desert sands of Canada." The fisher-folk have imaginations likely to be profoundly impressed by such harrowing tales, and the impression remains deep and vivid long after the arguments of common-sense have demonstrated its folly. Until further education and enlightenment is brought about, one can see how difficult it must be for the champions of confederation to persuade the fishermen that such a measure promises them greater happiness and prosperity.

I would as soon prefer to popularise a Prussian in the Vosges.

Newfoundland's curiously-isolated political condition—curiously isolated, in view of the confederation of all the other British North American colonies from the Atlantic to the Pacific—has perhaps puzzled people at a distance the most.

Why does the Tenth Island hold aloof? I had several talks with intelligent colonists on this subject. One of them said to me:

"The great obstacle is just this. Newfoundland stands on a different footing from the provinces which now form part of the Dominion, and we should expect altogether different terms. When British Columbia went into the federal union, the construction of the Canadian Pacific Railway to the coast was part of her bargain with Canada. If we had gone into confederation in 1869, a railroad across our island would have been one of our conditions."

"But you did not go in."

"No; the feeling of the people was that we did not want it. To-day it is true that confederation is not a live political issue with us. You find confederates and anti-confederates in the Ministry and in the Opposition; there is no dividing line on that issue, but nevertheless our people do at heart believe confederation to be their destiny—their inevitable destiny. Why? Well, there is the development of the colony, its geographical and political position; and indeed from whatever point of view the question is regarded, our manifest destiny is as part of the great Dominion of Canada. We alone stand outside now in all British North America. For our fishing population—and they, of course, form the bulk of our working-folk—it would be a great benefit. With the solitary exception of pork, which would still come from the United States, every article of diet for them would come in duty free from Canada. Our average import duties are now 30 per cent. You see what an advantage the abolition of those duties would be."

"You put political association with the United States out of the question."

"Yes, the United States does not come into the discussion at all. There was once a vague sort of talk of annexation and the rest of it, but Mr Cleveland's war Message killed what little there was of that—killed it absolutely. Directly the head of the American republic held up his fist to Old England, and talked war to her—that was enough for even the wildest annexationist we had, and he was really a mild specimen. We remembered our British stock, and you don't hear a whisper of annexation now. We are British stock—English, Irish, or Scotch descent; we are more proud of the fact than you in England would believe if I told you, and we mean to remain Britons to the end."

"And work out your destiny as part of the Great British federation of North America. On what terms?"

"Ah, that's the question. You had better ask Sir William Whiteway and his fellow-Ministers that, or rather perhaps, Sir Wilfrid Laurier and his colleagues, for it was at Ottawa that the negotiations fell through the other day. We should expect the Confederation to assume our debt—17,000,000 dols. As Canada built the Canadian Pacific Railway for British Columbia she should take our island railway into the account; it would have been charged to the Canadian general account had we gone into confederation in 1869. If that be taken out of our public debt it stands at between 9,000,000 and 10,000,000 dols., or about 50 dols. per head of our population, which is less than the proportion of the public debt of the Dominion. Let this allowance be made as the basis of the negotiations, and the rest should not be difficult.

"And, mind you, our financial position looks much better to-day than it did at the time of the last confederation negotiations. Our bonds are above par, and our revenue for the fiscal year ending June 30th show an increase of 130,000 dols. on the corresponding period of the preceding year. After the Bank crash stocks got low, and have now had to be replenished, while the increase of 5 per cent. on the tariff also materially assisted the revenue."

The fisherman is to the stranger the personification of hospitality. He is a great, warm-hearted fellow, whose bed and board and good offices are all at your disposal. I did not meet a single surly fisherman in Newfoundland, although I have met many such in other parts of the world where fishermen are congregated. In his hut, cabin, or cottage everything you see you may count upon as belonging to you for the time being; but be careful not to express a wish for anything you see, or no deprecations will prevent your coming out with it in your pocket or over your shoulder. In this connection I heard of a Yankee comedian who came to Newfoundland during the shooting season, being much struck by the extraordinarily and picturesquely patched trousers his host wore. "I shall have a pair like that," he exclaimed jocosely, and jotted down a few notes as to their appearance. When he and his companion had finished their meal and were turning to go, their hostess, in her lord's absence, pressed a parcel upon them which they accepted, thinking it was fish.

"Look here," said one of them when they had got well down the road, "I don't think we want this fish."

"We couldn't very well decline it. It's the custom here, I believe. I vote we give it to the first man we meet."

"Very well. I suppose," he added after a pause; "I suppose it *is* fish."

The parcel, being immediately opened, was found to contain the eccentric trousers. The two strangers ran back and took the fisherman completely by surprise. He was mending his nets, *in his wife's skirt*. It was a chilly day. He had been wearing those trousers for a period of seventeen years, and was naturally much hurt at the inability of his guest to accept the gift.

It is well not to express surprise if the interior of the hut or personal appearance of your host and his family is no indication, or at best but a slight one, of his worldly possessions. A leading banker of St John's said to me:

"Numbers of these fishermen are far from being poor men. Their habit of receiving always in gold and of paying always in kind led me to make enquiries; and my belief is that there is upwards of three million dollars at present hoarded along the south and east coasts. Many families which seem poor have tidy sums hidden in the chimney or cellar walls. To prove the practice, I may mention that many a fisherman, in paying off a mortgage, or setting up as a 'planter' or shipowner, will suddenly produce George IV. or King William guineas or sovereigns almost mint new, or bearing few marks of wear."

The fisherman, therefore, is an inheritor of the old peasant tradition that Banks are not to be trusted—a conviction which was certainly not weakened when the colony's Bank crash came in 1894, and noteholders and investors became penniless. In many a cottage of the outports, there must have been grim laughter and not a little dram-drinking when the tidings of the crash came out, and many complacent peeps at the yellow guineas gleaming by candle-light in the cellar.

Take him all round—his faults, his failings, his superstitions, and his personal uncleanliness and untidiness—and the fisherman is something more than the equal of most of the Anglo-Celtic offshoots. He is the superior of most. He is splendid physical raw material—a great tall strapping fellow—a pure blend, if ever there was one, of the English, Irish, and Scotch races. He is not intellectual, but there is good stuff in him—the very stuff England can ill afford to dispense with.

CHAPTER IX

It is one thing to catch your cod-fish: it is altogether another thing to sell him.

As the Banks of Newfoundland (those marine plateaux which I have previously described) are outside the limits of the colony's territorial waters, other nationalities, chiefly French and Americans, are engaged in the fishery there. It is the great increase of their numbers in late years, and the enormously increased quantity of fish thus obtained, which must also be regarded as one of the causes of the diminished prices which are seriously affecting the colony.

The panacea for this evil is more apparent than real. As the immediate neighbourhood of the coast of Newfoundland enables its people to cure even the fish caught on the Banks in such a manner as to better its quality and at a smaller cost than is possible for foreigners, the competition might assume equitable proportions, production in all probability declining until it had reached that point where it became remunerative for all concerned. But the competition is not a fair one. The advantages granted to the foreign fishermen by their respective Governments are such as to more than compensate for the natural advantages possessed by the people of Newfoundland. In a word, the former have been able to maintain and continually increase their products, while the latter are less and less able to maintain a struggle manifestly unequal.

America takes all the product of her fishermen caught on the Grand Banks, and imposes a duty of two shillings and fourpence a quintal on the fruits of British industry — thereby practically denying it her markets.

"The Americans," said a prominent Newfoundlander to me, "show a most selfish and contemptible spirit in their endeavour to get a share of our fisheries, whilst they keep us out of theirs, and exclude our fish production by prohibitive duties. Canada and Newfoundland —or, better still, Newfoundland and Canada— should follow Sir John MacDonald's policy, and show a firm front and determination to protect our fishery rights until the Americans give us a reciprocity treaty and free entry to their markets for our fish and all our natural products."

But the French Government not only prohibit absolutely the importation of British-caught fish into France, but by a system of export and other bounties, varying from eight to ten francs per quintal, actually support the French fishermen in their work of under-bidding the Newfoundlander in foreign markets.

Thus the American market is practically, and the French market actually, closed to British-caught fish, which, in addition, is being gradually forced out from all other markets except such countries as Brazil, which demand a quality which the French fishermen are unable to achieve, owing to the lack of curing facilities enjoyed by the Newfoundlanders.

By way of forcible illustration, French fish can be bought to-day all over the continent of Europe at 12s. 6d. a quintal—that is to say the French fishermen obtain for it 21s. a quintal—the bounty being thus equal to 72 per cent. of the value; while the British fishermen, for their superior produce, can obtain only 14s. a quintal, or 35 per cent. less.

In former years French cod-fish was unknown in various European waters, as the catch of the French was barely sufficient for the requirements of home consumption in France, but now the British Consuls in Italy and other parts of the Mediterranean, in Spain and Portugal, declare unanimously that the cheapness of the French fish is driving out the Newfoundland cure. As a proof of the utter impossibility of fair competition with French fish, it will suffice to mention the fact that French shippers have actually offered and sold fish to Spanish merchants in Bordeaux *for nothing*, the French shippers being satisfied with the bounty received from their Government. Competition cannot go much farther than this.

Is it proposed that the Newfoundland Government should retort by giving away a knife and fork with every cod-fish?

It will be seen, therefore, that the French fishery in relation to the colonists has undergone considerable change in recent years, to the colony's serious disadvantage. Formerly the bounty did not conflict with the island's interests, as the French "bankers" were equipped in France, and took most of their produce back to France to be consumed there, leaving only a small portion for exportation from St Pierre to the French West Indies. Consequently, Newfoundland seldom, if ever, found France a competitor in those markets to which she exported her fish.

Suddenly, as one might say, St Pierre has become an extensive port of trade and of export for traders from other countries. There is a large fleet of French bankers and also a fleet sailing under the French flag, managed by French agents at St Pierre, and owned to some extent by English and American subjects, employed in catching fish to compete with Newfoundland in all European markets. This is the spectacle of John Bull attempting to play

THE TENTH ISLAND

with the French at their own game. The increasing fleet of Bank fishers has an enormous advantage over the colonial fishermen, from the fact that, in addition to the bounty referred to, they obtain food and supplies of all kinds at St Pierre almost free of duty.

But it so happens—and here is the peg upon which the Newfoundland Government proposes to hang up the Frenchman—that the quantity of fish caught on the Banks depends very largely on the supply of fresh bait-fishes. These bait-fishes, caplin, squid, and herring, are principally obtained from the territorial waters of Newfoundland, being purchased by the foreigners from the fishermen of Fortune Bay and the neighbouring inlets. Salted and otherwise artificially-prepared bait, although capable of attracting cod, is far from being so efficacious. A fisherman with only salted bait at his command would soon fall far behind the others in his catch, no matter how fecund the waters might be. Fresh bait, therefore, if the supply from the neighbouring coast were closed to foreigners, could only be procured by them on the more distant portion of the Newfoundland coast where the French have fishing rights. If they went elsewhere it would be at great cost, and, owing to the ice, at a period of the year later by three or four weeks. Cut off the cheaper, readier, and steadier supply from the coast in the immediate neighbourhood of the Banks, and what would be the result? The result would be that, bounty or no bounty, the quantity obtained by foreigners would dwindle until it had fallen to that point when it would just suffice for their home markets. This being the case, it is evident that Newfoundland, by allowing foreigners to buy bait on her shores, has been all along furnishing the means of her own destruction to persons bent on ruining her by fair means or foul. Can it be doubted, then, that her only salvation lies in a measure which will regulate the sale of bait as it is regulated in England — which will prevent access to their coast of foreign fishermen whose fishing is not fair?

Goaded by the general hostile attitude of the French in other matters relating to the island, such as the Treaty shore and the smuggling from St Pierre, the Newfoundland Government passed in 1887 what is known as the Bait Bill. France, well instructed by its indefatigable agent, M. des Isles, spared no effort with the Imperial authorities to prevent the colony's passing the Bill. Without this defensive weapon the Tenth Island would soon be in the position of the sugar-exporting colonies of Barbados and Demarara, which are being rapidly ruined by the action of the foreign bounties.

Downing Street listened to the threats (vainly

disguised as protests) of the French Government, and withheld even its consideration of the colonial measure for several months. It then delivered itself in the following terms:—

"Her Majesty's Government would not be justified in disregarding the strong protest of the French Government against the introduction at this late period of restrictions calculated to inflict great loss upon the French fishermen; and as, for this reason, they are unable to advise the Queen to allow the Bill to come into law in respect of the approaching fishing season, it will not at present be submitted for Her Majesty's confirmation."

If we are driven to choose between offending the French and neglecting to care for the colonist, the colonist must go to the wall.

Were the loss occasioned to foreigners at all commensurate with that which was to be suffered in Newfoundland by its continuance, the argument against such a measure, on the ground of international comity, would, of course, have much force. As a matter of fact, one is not to be compared with the other. The fishing industry in the neighbourhood in question is, by comparison with other resources, of infinitesimal importance to the other peoples concerned. To the people of Newfoundland it is as yet their all in all. To withdraw the before-mentioned privilege from France would cause a comparatively trifling inconvenience. To continue it would mean our senior colony's ruin.

Even the Governor, Sir William Des Vœux, had written in these terms to the Colonial Office:

"I would respectfully express, on behalf of this suffering colony, the earnest hope that the vital interests of 200,000 British subjects will not be disregarded out of deference to the susceptibilities of any foreign Power, and this especially when the privilege which the Power desires to retain cannot be pretended to be matter of right, but is a benefit which may be lawfully withdrawn, as in the nature of a tenancy at will, and may now be justly withdrawn as being used for the infliction of fatal injury on those who have hitherto permitted its enjoyment."

When the colonists heard of the decision of the Colonial Office, their Legislature immediately framed and carried through another Bait Bill similar to the defunct measure, which they forwarded to the Mother Country with the hope that Her Majesty's Government would take due cognisance of the renewed effort.

"When we learn," said they, "from your despatch that the main reason for the refusal of our Bill is that its present adoption would 'inflict grave loss on the French fishermen,' we cannot forbear from the expression of our surprise at this apparent disregard of the

THE TENTH ISLAND

sufferings of our fishermen and of the British interests which are thus made subservient to the purposes of foreigners. The people of this colony have the right in our fisheries, and foreigners have not; and we cannot see those rights surrendered in defiance of our appeals without expressing our deep sense of the injustice to which our people are thus called on to submit." *

A delegation was sent to England, and after a great deal of agitation on one side and red tape on the other, the Bait Bill received Imperial sanction, and went into operation. But, as far as the absolute restriction of the sale of bait was concerned, the Act, as passed then, was not very efficacious through the lack of means taken to enforce it. It was a difficult job to persuade the poor fisherman that a bird in the hand was worth two in the bush. His patriotism and honour were appealed to. Here is one of the placards exhibited in a store-room at that time:

> THE FISHERMAN WHO WOULD
> SEL BATE TO
> A FRENCHMAN
> WOULD STEEL THE PENNY'S
> OFF HIS DEAD
> MOTHAR'S EYES!

* Address to the Secretary of State, February 21st, 1887.

Another ran thus:

> NEWFOUNDLANDERS, BE MEN!
> STARVE IF YOU MUST: BUT
> HANG ON TO YOUR HERRING!
>
> P.S.—If you sell bait to the French now you are bound to starve in the long Run.

Yet even with an imperfect enforcement the results were not ungratifying. The exports from St Pierre the two years following the passage of the Bait Act were as follow:—
In 1887 . . 754,770 quintals of 112 lbs. each.
„ 1888 . . 594,529 „ „ „
„ 1889 . . 299,273 „ „ „
I think, therefore, that I have shown the efficacy of the measure if it were properly carried out. But in 1890 came the lobster dispute on the French shore, and subsequently the Bait Act was repealed.

The Bait Act should again become law; but if it is to be carried out in such a half-hearted way as to give rise to the belief that it is a mere move in the political game, it had better never be passed. If the Bait Act is enforced in every outport in the colony, if every fisherman who transgresses its provisions is immediately made

THE TENTH ISLAND

to suffer a severe penalty, the situation is saved, and the evil of the French bounty system thwarted in the only effectual manner.

And the rigid enforcement of the Bait Act will have far-reaching consequences. By many it is regarded as the solution of all the questions relating to France and Newfoundland. The French set great store by their Bank fishery, which they declare, perhaps with their tongue in their cheek, is the nursery for their Navy, the most important source of recruiting of which is the *Marine de Commerce.* If, therefore, the main industry is crippled, France may be brought to that frame of mind which seeks for reasonable terms—for equitable compromise.

It is only fair to add that, in a short chat I had with an islander of bluff common-sense, Captain Delaney, he said to me bluntly:

"We can't afford to enforce the Bait Act. For one thing, Canada won't help us. Suppose we deny bait to the French, what is to prevent the Canadian selling it to him—coming over to our coasts, even, and buying it from our men, and then passing it on for a profit. Our law won't say our fishermen can't sell bait to Canadian fishermen: the only result will be that the profits of the bait business will pass from our hands into the hands of the Canadians."

"You won't get Canada to help Newfoundland," said another man, "until we get a statesman with more youth and backbone than old Bill Whiteway to ask her to help. As far as I can see at present, she will only help us beat the French if we become a part of the Dominion, and she won't let us join the Dominion until we have settled the French shore question! Now, what in hell are we going to do?"

Certainly the bait predicament is a curious one; and I was hardly prepared then to answer the question.

CHAPTER X

A SEAL in Newfoundland is, in common parlance, a "swile."

There are two days in March every year which are notable among the fisher-folk. One is St Patrick's Day—the other occurs five days earlier, when the sealing season begins. The sealing season is to the people of the Tenth Island what the shooting season is to the people of the "tight little island"—only more so. In order for the Twelfth of August to thoroughly resemble the Twelfth of March, it would be requisite that the stomachs and purses of Englishmen of town and country should be dependent on the results of the bagging of grouse and other game effected by the amateur Nimrods of Mayfair.

"Cruel sports," remarks a famous writer, "do not make a cruel people." Clearly cruel occupations do not. Still, even admitting the Chicago pig-sticker to be the "mildest-mannered man that ever cut a throat"; the *employé de l'abattoir* to be a person of sensibility and peace; even then, I cannot quite fathom the gentleness and humanity of the Newfoundland seal-hunter. He has every reason to be a cold-blooded monster, dead to every emotion of mercy and pity. When

I say that the annual seal hunt of Newfoundland is one great carnival of cruelty and bloodshed, I say that which not every witness to, but every participant in, its horrors readily admits. Yet I never saw or heard of but one man who shrank from the slaughter. That man told me, in his own quaint fashion, that he woke up one night and discovered himself standing over the bed of his crying child with a sealing gaff in his hand.

"S' help me, God," he said, "I didn't sleep an honest sleep for many nights after that. I never heard the kid cry without thinkin' first off o' the whimper o' them 'swiles'; an' how near I'd come to killin' my own flesh an' blood. I tried to laugh it off, but it was no use; and so when the 'swiler' came to start I give my place to another man. I knew after that I was no good for 'swilin'' any more—faith, the gaff would ha' fallen out o' my hands."

After the cod-fish, the sealing industry ranks next in importance in the Tenth Island. It must be understood that that seal, the capture of which is of such value to the Tenth Island, is not at all the seal known to the fur trade. It is the oil seal, whose hide is used for the manufacture of a coarse-grained leather, called technically by various misnomers. His fat furnishes an oil very much in demand for illuminating and lubricating purposes, and also for the manufacture of soap. "Seal soap" has a decidedly taking sound, but I fear, after the description I am about to give of the manner of the animal's capture, it will scarcely command a large sale among persons of feeble nerves and strong sensibilities.

The seal-hunt is a comparatively modern occupation for the inhabitants. For three hundred years, during which the cod-fishery was prosecuted, the Arctic seals were left to bring forth their young upon the distant ice-floes, and there was no organised attempt to invade them with the murderous weapons of the seal-hunter. But the seal was not for ever to enjoy such immunity. Ninety years ago the first hunters forced their way through the icy ramparts where he and his young were ensconced, and came upon what may be described as a huge Arctic seal nursery. There were thousands and thousands of small floes, and upon every floe reclined a small brood of infant seals. From that day the slaughter began; and a mighty new industry opened up for the Newfoundland fishermen.

According to law, no sealing vessel can leave port until March 12th, but it is two days later before any seals can be killed—a regulation framed to protect the premature killing of seals.

The majority of the populations of the outports come to see them off and to wish them luck. The steamers appear to be packed from stem to stern with humanity—patched, weather-beaten, greasy humanity—all shouting and cheering and waving their caps and sou'westers. Many a man who has shipped aboard one of these sealing steamers for the sake of the experience has lived to regret it. The huddling together in filth of 350 men in a small boat for five or six weeks, without room to lie down and rest—men standing elbow to elbow and swallowing their food like dogs—is a scandal already stirring the colony. But I will deal with that presently.

It is the object of the skipper to reach the baby seals as quickly as possible and secure his cargo before the beginning of April. For by that date the seals are old enough to take to the water and make their escape. If the crew is in luck, and there is not too much ice afloat, on the third or fourth day a seal-patch is sighted and the whimpering of the countless young seals is heard. This cry, which so tickles the crew that they can hardly restrain their delight, bears an awful resemblance to the sobbing of a human infant in pain. The vessel is laid-to, and the crew are out upon the ice in a jiffy, each man armed with his iron-shod gaff and sharp knife. On all sides, as far as the eye can see, are the white-coated seals, often attended by the mother-seals, whose maternal instinct is very strong, the tenderness with which the mothers watch over their offspring being really touching. It is stated that when the young are cradled on the ice the mothers go off each morning to fish, returning at intervals to give them suck. The destruction begins quite without prelude. One or two blows on the head fractures the skull of the young seal, if the gaff be in the hands of an old sealer. The others of the group are treated in like fashion, to the chorus of heart-rending cries and sobs. Almost at the same moment the knife is brought into play, and the skin and fat detached from the carcases, which, still quivering with life—often struggling, and occasionally still whimpering—are instantly surrounded by the miserable mother. Her moans, as it gazes upon the sickening, moving red masses, all that is left of her children, are fearful to hear.

It is now the rude details of the slaughter-house over again. Clots of gore cover the hands and limbs, and even the faces, of the men; the ice is stained and slippery with mingled blood and fat; the air reeks with the smell of blood, and still that low human whimper goes up, and the slaughter goes on. It is the slaughter-house, but what pen or abattoir ever had such surroundings as these: the calm silent whiteness of the snow, the stately purity of the icebergs, whose thousand cathedral-like spires and pinnacles glitter in the sun, are little in accord with the bloody nature of this industry.

But if the scene of the actual slaughter is not calculated to please and agreeably stimulate the feelings, what can one say of the state of things which quickly prevails on board the steamer itself? The men are now busily dragging in their "pelts," and throwing them into heaps in the hold. When the hold is filled, as it is after a day or two, they throw them into the forecastle and the cabins; and when these in turn are full, they pile them on the decks. Then they sleep on them, if they care to, their garments saturated with blood and fat. The stench is horrible.

The hunters are still scattered over the ice in all directions, and some have wandered miles from the ship. It is a business not without peril, but these men seem as oblivious to the dangers of drowning or being crushed to death by ice as one of the seals themselves. Not seldom the field-ice upon which they are engaged breaks up suddenly into fragments, and they are floated off to fill watery graves. Occasionally a violent storm arises, and the steamer, with its freight, is caught between icebergs. During the seal-hunt of 1872 one hundred men perished. But, after all, the most fearful thing in connection with sealing is the awful experience of living aboard a sealing steamer during the period—from four to six weeks—that she is out from port. Since the evils arise from overcrowding, why, one naturally asks, are so many men taken on board?

I was told that one reason is that more than twice as many men as can be taken are eagerly pressing for berths at the shipping offices, and begging and praying to be permitted to go. Some of them, the young especially, like the excitement and adventure of the hunt with all its hardships, for if they return successful they are the heroes of the hour; but with the great bulk it is "their poverty, not their will," that forces them on board. There are empty cupboards and hungry mouths at home, and the hope of returning with "a good bill" makes them submit to any conditions. But there is another reason. The owners of the steamers naturally want to bring in as many seals as possible. Should a steamer with a large number of men on board strike the "seal-patch," she will be quickly and certainly loaded; and in any case, with a large crew the chances of success are multiplied; and so, between the poverty of the men and the greed of the owners, the disreputable and injurious practice goes on. It is marvellous how few accidents occur. The captains can pick their men, and take only the younger and the hardier. Disease on board is infrequent; but this year five dead bodies were brought home by the fleet. Sickness and death on board a sealing steamer are enough to appeal to the stoutest heart. Should an epidemic break out on board one of these over-crowded vessels the results would be terrible. One of them was reported to have had diphtheria on board this year. If strong measures are not taken, some frightful disaster may occur; for should a vessel strike a rock, the boats would not contain more than half the crew if she were to sink. And yet the chief opponents of any reduction of the crews would be the men themselves!

One of the ablest and most experienced sealing skippers, Captain Samuel Blandford, feels, I am very glad to say, very strongly on this matter. In nineteen years this captain has landed 332,278 seals, the highest record, so that his remarks carry weight.

"Go on board one of the sealing steamers," said he, "and visit the forecastle and other parts of the ship. Only look where Christians have to live, huddled away together in filth, and without room even to lie down to take rest—men standing elbow to elbow and swallowing their food like dogs. Only imagine 375 men crowded together in one ship. The condition of such a sealing crew is simply indescribable; and no other Christian country in the world would tolerate such a condition of things in view of the dangers attending such a voyage. It was high time that something were done to protect the interests and lives of our fellow-countrymen. There was a law regulating the carrying of cattle on shipboard, and yet in a matter where the lives of hundreds of our fishermen were concerned it was regarded as not being of any importance whatever that they should be provided with the protection that would be given even to dumb animals."

The lives and interests of the sealers should certainly be the first consideration with those who profess to be so interested in the welfare of the colony. The owners of steamers claim they cannot very well prevent the overcrowding, as there are 15,000 men in the country anxious to get to the seal-fishery, and it is hard under certain circumstances to refuse applicants for berths. Still, contends the captain, it is wrong to carry from 300 to 400 men just for the sake of giving an extra number something to eat for the time being. It was the last forty or fifty men taken that caused all the trouble and over-crowding and risk of life on board the steamers. In the over-crowded vessels there were always from forty to fifty men sick or disabled and this was the result of over-crowding. The ships were well fitted and well provisioned, but it was not much use to the men when they had not even elbow or standing room, and were forced to take their food under worse conditions than the dumb animals.

Others who have been many years in the seal fishery and have witnessed the hardships and risks to life to which the men were exposed, express themselves as ready to do whatever was in their power to bring about a proper remedy and to protect the men. It is in their opinion a shame and a disgrace to civilisation that human beings should be left with scarcely any protection and be less cared for than the animals on board cattle ships. Why should 1000 men be privileged by being allowed to go to the seal fishery to the disadvantage and inconvenience of 4000? It was a ruinous and dangerous practice, and the sooner the number of the crews were limited by law the better.

"I have gone," continued Captain Blandford, "down into the fo'castle of the *Neptune* to see sick persons, and have been almost suffocated during the few moments I have been there; it is a wonder to me how the crews existed at all under such circumstances."

Altogether, I think the reader will agree that sealing and the conditions attending its prosecution are among the least attractive things to be said about the Tenth Island.

CHAPTER XI

THE colony, in spite of its meagre population, has all the equipment of a good-sized nation. In the machinery of its Government is comprehended not only the Governor, the usual executive departments, and two legislative bodies, but a constabulary, a postal service, a force of revenue officers, lighthouse keepers, road-masters, etc.; while among the assets of the colony are roads, railways, lighthouses, docks, and public buildings adequate to serve for a country of ten times its numerical importance.

The colony derives almost the whole of its revenue from customs duties on imports. These duties are partly *ad valorem* and partly specific; but, although the tariff is professedly for revenue only, there are a number of differential duties: and if the Government thought there were any further industries worthy of protection, I do not doubt they would find it in their hearts to protect them. The revenue averages about 1,700,000 dols. annually; and out of this sum are defrayed the expenses of the colony and the payment of interest on its debt. Last year, I was informed by Mr Scott, the Receiver-General, there was, owing to the new policy of retrenchment in expenditure, a surplus of 200,000 dols.

The members of the Opposition are not very sanguine about the continuance of that surplus.

"It's too good to last," said one man. "It was unintentional, and I'll take a bet that next year there'll be a deficit of 200,000 dols. to make it up. As to their retrenchment—why, already they're putting back every item in the Budget they cut off."

At present there are no direct taxes in the colony, except a municipal tax in St John's for water, light, sewerage, and street improvements.

The public debt is represented chiefly by the lines of railway, and also by the St John's dry dock and the new post-office.

Representative government was granted to Newfoundland in 1832. Twenty-three years later England conceded to the colony that system of Responsible Government whereby she herself is governed, which consists in the victors at the polls being accorded the offices and appointments in the colony. The party in power selects the executive council. Of the two houses, the House of Assembly (thirty-six members) is elected by the people; the Legislative Council (fifteen members) is nominated by the Governor in Council and serve for life.

The Governor is appointed by the Crown.

The Governor's salary, which, in the opinion

of many persons, constitutes the most practical tie between the island of Newfoundland and the island of England, is paid by the colony. Up to the time of the recent financial difficulties this salary was 12,000 dols., but in 1894 a great fever of retrenchment swept over the colony. Officials were docked right and left: two portfolios were rolled into one, and every petty clerk and Government servant was made to share the pecuniary embarrassment of the State.

It is needless to say that the viceregal "screw" did not escape the chisel of reform.

Now, £2400 cannot be regarded as anything but a moderate income for such a post; but £1400 is manifestly inadequate. Good men cannot be got at such a figure. My belief is that Newfoundland should be regarded as outside the circle of ordinary governorships. Its importance is greater than its population implies: and the need of a first-rate man larger than the inducements offered him to rule the colony. At one time it entered the head of the Colonial Office to allow the island to be governed by one of its own public men. Sir Ambrose Shea, a Newfoundlander by birth and descent, and a capable man in every way, and who had been administrator in the absence of the Governor, happened to be in London in 1887, in connection with the Colonial Conference.

He was offered, and accepted, the Governorship. Elated by the honour, he cabled out to a relative in the colony the tidings of his appointment. The news spread like wild-fire. Instead of being received with enthusiasm, it was greeted with the utmost indignation. Even Sir Ambrose Shea's best friends turned against him. "Old Awmber Shea gettin' 12,000 dols. a year?" exclaimed one old fisherman. "Sure, there'd be a riot from here to Labrador if it was tould that one of our own boys, raised right here amongst us, was drawin' 12,000 dols. a year!" Petitions were signed by the leading citizens, from the Supreme Court of Justice downwards, remonstrating against the appointment. The consequence was that the Imperial Secretary was obliged to bow before the storm. He had no other resource but to beseech Sir Ambrose to save the situation by declining the appointment. It only remains to mention that, by way of solatium, Sir Ambrose was given the Governorship of the Bahamas, which he filled for two terms with signal success.

To return to the Governor's salary, the Colonial Office has temporarily found a way out of the difficulty of getting a capable man at the reduced figure, by taking the present Governor out of the Customs, and increasing his pension to £1000 and thereby making up the deficiency. What course they will adopt with Sir Herbert Murray's successor, supposing there is not another sturdy old gentleman in the Customs who is possessed of an amiable inclination to emigrate, I shall be obliged to leave to conjecture.

The Legislature meets once a year, usually in February. A shrewd, well-spoken fellow, with a taste for politics, can become a member of the House of Assembly—if he play his cards aright. Truckling to the fishermen is not a nice game—but there is an excitement about it not often obtained elsewhere. There are 18 electoral districts, sending 36 members to the House as follows:—

	Members
Bay-de-Verds	2
Bonavista	3
Burgee and La Paile	1
Burin	2
Carbonear	1
Ferryland	2
Fogo	1
Fortune Bay	1
Harbour Grace	3
Harbour Main	2
Placentia and St Mary's	3
Port de Grave	1
St Barbe	1
St George	1
St John's East	3
St John's West	3
Trinity	3
Twillingate	3
Total	36

Let us imagine a moderate-sized hall, whose mural bareness suggests a barn, packed with a motley humanity. On a platform at the farther end are seven men, six of whom are seated on chairs. The room is badly lighted by swinging kerosene lamps, rather leaky, one of which is placed immediately over the head of the seventh man, who looks a little out of place amid his surroundings, but who appears to be doing his best to achieve a consonance by dint of base rhetoric.

"What have they done — these polysyllable patriots — these men who polysyllabically profess to," etc. "Let me tell you, gentlemen, that treachery, duplicity, and mendacity will not save," etc. "That reminds me of a story once told by the great Daniel O'Connell," etc. "And do they dare with this odoriferous record of cowardice and deceit to come before the free and enlightened," etc.

The odour of the place is reprehensible. Almost from the first, a dozen tiny streams of tobacco juice course tortuously between the seats, and by degrees reach the aisle; and a current visible to all, swollen from a hundred sources, courses silently to the door. Notwithstanding the prohibition "No Smoking," a dozen pipes are emitting smoke furtively in the corners.

The speaker warms up to his work. But in

THE TENTH ISLAND

the height of his ardour he never loses the restraint of polysyllables. He calls the Opposition by every compound at his command, a practice which seems to be relished by the poor fishermen. Of the seven men on the platform, only four wear white linen collars, which demonstrates that these four are men of standing in the community.

At last the audience begin to exhibit impatience, and the candidate having finished his speech, the chairman, who is none other than our old friend, Mr Thomas Codlin, calls upon Mr Patrick Bailey. Whereat there is good humour and great cheering, and a fusilade of facetious remarks levelled at the new speaker. It is equally clear that Mr Patrick Bailey is a person of some distinction, and the possessor of a fund of common-sense and rough humour. In marked distinction to the somewhat refined appearance of the last speaker, he has a large, florid face, a careless attire, and a somewhat thick brogue. He is a lawyer in St John's, a member of the Government, and one of the most popular and best known men in the island. His loyalty to the Crown is unquestionable, his ability beyond dispute; and if he were more crafty, less honest, and less popular, there is little doubt that this poor fisherman's son would some day become Premier. For Patrick Bailey's father may be seen any day in the streets of a certain out-harbour, ready to tell of the day when his lad, then a "sprat of a boy," threw down the fishing net and lines and said:

"Father, it's a lawyer I'm afther becoming. His reverence says it's more I'll make out o' my book-learning than I'll get out o' the fish. And so, beggin' your leave, I'm done with it."

A little later Patrick was employed in the office of a St John's lawyer in good practice, for the fishermen are litigious—picking up a good deal during the day, and being taken in hand by a certain benevolent priest during the evening. It was years of this sort of thing which gave Pat Bailey those narrow shoulders and that stoop which go so ill with his big frame and large, florid head. Yet he grew up to be a rough, hearty Irishman, tempered by industry and sobriety. He went into politics soon after he was called to the Bar; and he knows the fisherman and his tastes and desires as well, if not better, than any man in the island. He has fought some curious battles, and taken part in some curious adventures. He has gone down into the outports, and slept and smoked, eaten and drunk with the poorest and roughest fishermen. He has told them funny stories, flirted with their wives and daughters, "argeyfied" with the priest, had hand-to-hand physical conflicts with rowdies bent on breaking up his meetings, played "mummers," caught fish, and

THE TENTH ISLAND

in the end beaten his opponent where nobody besides Pat Bailey would have got twenty votes.

He has now come down into Twillingate to help elect the son of a brother lawyer, who was educated in England, and who cannot relate brutal stories and look burly and rubicund as to the manner born. For the great point about Pat Bailey is that the fishermen regard him as one of themselves. His stories bring shrieks of laughter, and "Pat's latest joke" is one of the standing topics in the island.

In the Legislature the Honourable Patrick Bailey is an altogether different being. His manner is grave and earnest. He advocates all measures directed towards the good of the island, but he never enthuses over any speculative project. He appears to have little of the Irish imagination, and when anybody speaks of the future of Newfoundland, its gleaming agricultural possibilities, its mineral wealth, or its railway, he adopts a sceptical attitude or changes the subject. One of his favourite remarks is: "I don't want to hear about our undeveloped resources; I want to know what you are doing with your developed resources."

The members of the Legislature are paid. Assembly men, if resident in St John's, receive 194 dols. a session; if resident elsewhere, 291 dols.; a scale the principle of which is not so obvious. The legislative councillors receive 120 dols. a session, the President 240 dols. The salary of the Speaker of the House of Assembly is 1000 dols. a session.

It is rare to find a Government in Newfoundland hang well together. There is always a great deal of inter-official jealousy, and not that sense of subordination to a master-mind which guarantees strength to Cabinets. Every man seems bent on playing his own hand, and getting as much credit for himself as possible. The factor that knits them closest together is the patronage and thinly-veiled contempt of the Governor. I am told that he is accustomed to summon an executive council of the Cabinet, listen to all their views on any impending question, and then, without condescending to express his own, proceed, on the departure of his constitutional advisers, to act as if their advice had never been given. All this does not tend to increase his popularity, and, as the Government is careful to saddle him with the odium of all objectionable measures, the Governors of Newfoundland have rarely ever been popular. The present Premier told me that he had to exert all his authority to prevent a hostile demonstration against one recent Governor. Popular outbursts against the executive are not uncommon in St John's, and Government House has more than once been attacked. It is certain that with so stubborn and "touchy" a people as the St John's people the way to popularity is not easy. Yet it would seem that common prudence would have suggested to him that the executive action I am going to relate was unwise. It is the custom, on the adjournment or prorogation of the Legislature, for the Government to prepare a Queen's Speech, the draft of which is submitted to the Governor for his approval. At the last session the prepared speech contained several such passages as this: "You have *well and faithfully* performed your duties," etc.

The Governor very calmly, and in the presence of his Cabinet, dips his pen in red ink, and deletes the italicised phrases.

Whereupon he smiles a pleasant smile, returns the address to his discomfited advisors, and proceeds to open the parcel of the *Times* newspaper, which has just arrived from England, with every appearance of interest.

CHAPTER XII

AN essay on the county roads of Newfoundland would be almost as short as the memorable one on the snakes in Ireland.

In the first place, there are no counties in Newfoundland, and roads but recent innovations. Seventy years ago there were nothing but pathways, and few of these, as all communication was carried on by water. The inhabitants have since been bestirring themselves, and now roads and road-making occupy a considerable portion of the time, thoughts, energies, and capital of the colony.

There are three distinct lines of railway in Newfoundland, all constructed since 1882. The line which runs from St John's to Whitbourne, of which Sir Francis Evans, M.P., was recently president, joins at the latter station the great Newfoundland railway. At present the islanders are naturally not great travellers; one train each way daily suffices for the traffic. On the great railway across the island there are as yet but three trains a week.

The rolling-stock is of the American pattern. The cars strike one as a combination of the English and American systems. The long carriage is divided into first and second classes, but no smoking is permitted first-class. This rule, however, began to lapse as we proceeded farther and farther into the interior. Habits of constraint also began to relax, and before that long journey of thirty hours was over many of us had entirely lost sight of the distinction we bore as first-class passengers, and comported ourselves in a very third-class fashion indeed. I know that the solitary car speeding through the wilderness began to fill up with sportsmen and labourers; and that I slept that night with my feet resting in the lap of one gentleman, whose feet were in the lap of my neighbour.

After leaving St John's the train runs westward through rather a pretty interesting country, as far as Conception Bay, fifteen miles from the capital. Here is located Topsail, a pleasant village on the shores of this splendid bay, and at present a favourite summer and bathing resort for the St John's people. I was told by a physician here that the air, even in the hottest summer months, is always cool and bracing. Topsail, therefore, with its ethereal, topographical, and marine appointments, would make its fortune either in Europe or America; but as the mountain cannot go to Mahomet, the health and holiday seeking multitudes of the States who desire a real change would do well to consider Topsail. But one thing I should strongly advise the Newfoundlanders to do. Nature has indeed been lavish to them in what are termed "summer resorts"; but unless they can devise some way to speedily erect hotels and secure a series of landlords—both in the capital and elsewhere—tourists will shun their shores with great singleness of purpose. Here is an excellent opportunity for the Gordon Hotels Company, or those enterprising persons who erect such enormous hydropathic establishments as those at Crieff and Callander, to extend somewhat the field of their operations. The scenery from the carriage windows, as the train winds along the shores of the bay, is really very fine.

I was rather curious concerning the profuse shrubbery of this district—and, indeed, I found it to characterise the entire island. Wherever the eye turns it encounters the wild whortle or blue-berry bush; and, indeed, wild berries of every description, including strawberries and raspberries. The great profusion of this fruit has suggested to some enterprising individual to gather and manufacture preserves from them. He made a good beginning by forwarding a large parcel of preserved wild Newfoundland berries to the Queen, who graciously acknowledged them.

After Whitbourne, the country from the car windows grows brown and barren. Now and then one comes across a great patch, several miles square, of agricultural country — only waiting to be tilled. The forests are chiefly spruce, although balsam, poplar, and elder are frequent. Lakes, almost invariably called ponds, and rivers are too common to attract notice. Some of the scenery, as we turn a bend, is superb.

It is all Norway over again, but there never were so many lakes or so much inland water before in the world. One-third of the whole area of the island is water.

Soon one gets more into the country: and it becomes easier to take one's bearings.

In its course from Red Indian Lake downwards the Exploits River receives the waters of eight tributaries, the largest being Great Rattling Brook, Chute, Sandy and Badger Brooks, while four large streams discharge into the river itself. I will not attempt to enumerate the host of smaller streams. The main river valley from Red Indian Lake downwards, is, nearly for the whole distance, a level or gently-undulating country, broken only by occasional abrupt hills or rocky eminences, and densely wooded for many miles back from either bank of the stream. I say densely wooded; but I do not mean stunted Norwegian firs or dwarfed Iceland pines. The forests of the Exploits Valley consist of pine, spruce, balsam, fir, tamarack, white birch, and poplar. I soon found that the old tradition which represents the island as incapable of producing trees except of small size and stunted growth is, like many others, false. In many parts of the island as well as here are great forests, where the average girth of the trees is not much, if anything, under nine feet. I saw a number of trees which I should take to be three or four feet in diameter; and these, besides, ran straight up for fifty feet without a branch or knot.

At Norris's Arm, by the beautiful Exploits River, where we made a halt for refreshment, there is an hotel, and there we found quite a party of sportsmen. This is the head-quarters of the deer-slayer. The station-master is a little man, somewhat lame, with a great taste for music. I shall always carry with me a remembrance of his impromptu concert, in which he played the zither à *merveille*. When I resumed my journey I fell into conversation with an American, who comes often to the colony for sport. We talked about everything —but chiefly the French shore question.

"I guess they've been run pretty close to secession point," he said.

"Do you think there is any annexation sentiment? Will Newfoundland ever join the United States?"

He eyed me narrowly. When he saw my query was downright earnest, he bit off a

THE TENTH ISLAND 135

small piece of tobacco (a habit doubtless acquired in Newfoundland), and said:—" Of course, America's a free and glorious country, but I guess there's about as much chance of Newfoundland joining the United States as of the Gulf of St Lawrence running dry. They'll leave the country, and as a matter of fact, a lot of them do every year, but as soon as they can get money enough back they'll come. America would be ashamed to treat a dependency as England has treated Newfoundland. They've been sat on and pushed aside and neglected right and left. Is that the way France treats St Pierre?"

"No," my American friend went on, "the fact is, Newfoundlanders are proud to consider themselves Englishmen. Families whose bone and sinew have been made in the island these two hundred years talk of going home—to England. Take the police force of St John's. They speak of them there as Her Majesty's guardians of the peace. When the Queen's Birthday comes round every year, it's a sight to see all those fishermen and tradesmen and merchants waving their Union Jacks, and firing off their cannon, and ringing bells, especially when you know that they owe it to themselves that their island isn't a vast howling wilderness, or else handed over bodily to France."

Here our conversation was interrupted by the

report that a herd of two hundred deer were crossing the track in front of the train. Whereat the train stopped, and, it is unnecessary to add, most of our sportsmen took leave of us.

The caribon or reindeer are finer than the similar breed of Norway. Stags have been often shot weighing forty stone and more. I have seen antlers with fifty-two points. The antlers of these caribon are palmated, sweeping backward, and of superb proportions, the broad antlers meeting over the nose, as one writer says, "like a pair of hands clasped in the attitude of prayer." The migrations of these deer, who shed their horns in November, are as regular as the seasons. With the first October frosts they turn their heads southwards from the Bonne Bay country, where they feed and bring forth their young, arriving in the southern districts up to November. The best shooting months are September and October; but the fishermen on the southern shore seem to get good shooting well into the winter, for they make incursions into the interior and bring back many hundreds of carcases. At times the St John's market is positively flooded in winter with venison hailing from this quarter. The flesh often brings as little as five cents a pound. Deer-shooting, since the new railway, is getting to be, for the average man, a moderately inexpensive sport;

but in the days when Lord Dunraven went on his shooting tour, some fifteen years ago, it was an undertaking of no mean pretensions. It is still necessary to have somebody in the party with a pretty good knowledge of the habits of the deer, as well as a couple of Micmac Indian guides. Lord Dunraven summed up the sporting situation by saying that the caribou were plentiful, and the "Newfoundland stags are finer by far than any to be found in any portion of the North American continent." "Fur," he declared, "is pretty plentiful, wild fowl and grouse abundant, and the creeks and rivers are full of salmon and trout." On the whole, one can safely affirm that there is no country so near England which offers a similar prospect of good sport as Newfoundland. And under the new conditions, which promise to alter the face of the colony, such sport cannot go on but for a definite period.

At the Stone Quarries we partook of a repast with the workmen. The experience was one to be remembered as long as stomach lasts!

We sat down to a long plank table, eight on a side, and ate from tin plates and drank from the cups. I will not describe what we ate, although I shall carry a recollection of each item with me to my grave. It was the tea, and the tea alone, which transfixed me, first with horror, and then with an irresistible fascination. Tea in Newfoundland is boiled. When it has boiled it is taken out and reboiled. At the seventh stooping the tea has taken on those qualities for which tea is (in Newfoundland) esteemed.

The Quarries' tea is often kept boiling seven months! That is to say, what has been put into the cauldron in April is still sizzling merrily in October.

Our train was soon approaching a wide and beautiful river—the Humber. It is extensively wooded on both sides, and is the richest and most fertile country I had yet seen in the island.

To the north, as one approached Bay of Islands, a glimpse can be caught of an enormous tract of prairie grass, four or five feet high, and miles in extent. This grass for the most part cured on its stalk, and in winter would provide fodder for many thousand head of cattle. Not only are hundreds of square miles uninhabited, but even unexplored, save by the countless herds of wild deer.

Bay of Islands, the temporary terminus of the railway, is one of the most beautiful places I have ever visited. The first thing that arrests the attention is the extreme blueness of the great sheet of water which bursts upon the view. It is as blue as the waters of the Mediterranean; it is almost as blue as the Bay of Havana; and that is the bluest expanse I know of. The next thing that strikes you is the altitude of the surrounding mountains—the Blomidon range—many of whose peaks reach 2000 feet. The bay is dotted with numerous islands. The sound of cascades dropping hundreds of feet down the sheer sides of the half-encircling sierras, the majesty of the sunrise and sunset, the refreshing verdure which everywhere meets the eye, all proclaim a spot which is sanctified by Dame Nature, and deserves something better of mankind than obscurity. I did not visit Boune Bay; but I was told by Mr Fisher (to whose daughter I beg to present my best remembrances—her repast of venison and ptarmigan was delicious) that its scenery was the equal, if not superior, to that of Bay of Islands.

A steamer or two plies along the coast; and it was by steamer that I visited Bay St George and Port-aux-Basques, and at both places I had talks with the fishermen. Here I found them all hotly in favour of confederation, and at Channel they wanted me to make a speech. They were particularly exercised about the existing law concerning the magistracy of the coast, the duties of which are now undertaken by the British naval officer. The colonists want their own local judges to arbitrate in all the affairs of the district, or else the appointment of an Imperial judge. I cannot refrain from relating the following incident as it was related to me:—

A few weeks ago the captain of a French vessel

came ashore, got drunk, and committed a very grave assault. A band of citizens, with the authority of the local magistrates, set off in pursuit, with the intention of arresting the offender and incarcerating him, pending the arrival of the British naval officer. But the criminal escaped, and the whole affair, being reported to the officer, he used these words:—

"I am very glad that your purpose was frustrated. Had you apprehended the captain for this crime, it might have caused unpleasant relations between Great Britain and France."

Port-aux-Basques is an extraordinary little place—a bare rock, where a single tree or green thing is never seen—yet where scores of happy laughing children scamper to and from school, with nothing apparently to grace their lives, confronted by nothing from dawn till dark but the rude details of fishing and what the priest teaches them; and yet happy with the mere joy of living. All mankind, I suppose, is that way until the grey surliness of life and landscape puts out its spiritual sunshine. The fresh complexions and naïve manners of the lads and lasses were highly exhilarating, and I was glad that the new railway was to come this way and open the world to their romping eyes. For it is into this ineffably dreary, bleak little winding place on the rocks that the railway is to come and build its terminus. Port-aux-Basques, which has been sleeping heavily with its dried fish for centuries, is to become the town of Channel—perhaps the city of Channel. And when the Channel Brass Band is playing before its Town Hall, and the tired citizens are parading its esplanade, I shall, if I live to see the day, think of the flaxen-haired maiden who had never seen a tree, a brick house, or a lamp-post, and who kissed her little brown fingers to me as the steamer sailed away.

CHAPTER XIII

CINDERELLA is rather embarrassed with land. She has more of it than she knows what to do with — for, apart from the peninsula of Avalon, there are perhaps six persons in the island who solely follow the vocation of farmer. In spite of the fact that a third of its surface is lakes and rivers, and a great deal of swamp and arid territory, there are no less than seven thousand square miles of agricultural land in the Tenth Island unsettled. In other words, there are more than twenty thousand free farms, and no takers.

As a proof of what Newfoundland can do in the agricultural way, I may quote from Sir Stephen Hill, who was Governor in 1873, and who says that "the agricultural capabilities of the island are far greater than are usually assigned to it, and that large portions are capable of a high cultivation. The area of the fertile portions added together amount to many millions of acres. With respect to the products of the colony, potatoes, turnips, cabbages, peas, beans, and indeed all vegetables which grow in England, arrive at the highest state of perfection in Newfoundland. Of cereals,

its barley and oats will not suffer by comparison with the produce of Nova Scotia. . . .
As regards fruit, currants, strawberries, gooseberries, and cherries, with other fruit, grow in the gardens, and countless species of berries are found in great profusion throughout the country."

After this, an Englishman, one of those whose cardinal belief has been from childhood that Newfoundland is a fog-bound rock, may well rub his eyes in astonishment. I shall never forget my own amazement when I first came upon the coloured poster in St John's announcing the Annual Agricultural Show.

I think I should have experienced the same emotion had I been caught in a snow-storm in Barbados.

It is certainly no little exploit that a society of fifty or sixty members should organise such an agricultural show as this, in which prizes of 500 dols., besides the usual array of silver trophies, medals, and so forth, are offered. By these annual exhibits in every branch of the farmers' industry it has been clearly shown that even on the peninsula of Avalon, "which is quoted by all authorities as being the least productive portion of the island," splendid livestock, root crops, fruit, and even cereals worthy of a place in any Sussex or Devonshire show can be produced. At the last exhibition there were over a thousand entries for produce and live stock. There were cabbages weighing from 30 to 40 lbs. each; turnips, twenty to the barrel; and fine specimens of beet, carrots, and parsnips. The separate exhibition of dairy products was equal to anything in a town of similar size in Canada.

Of course, when one speaks, as I do here, of the agricultural accomplishments of Newfoundland, it must be remembered that, as yet, only the poorest portions of the soil of the island have been brought under cultivation, and those least favoured by climate. The very worst land is that in the neighbourhood of St John's; so that, if this district can make such an excellent showing, it may be left to the imagination to depict what must happen when the four or five million acres of rich fertile soil in the interior of the island are opened up by the plough. Much has already been said of the causes which have retarded the agricultural progress of the colony up to the present moment—the early prohibition of settlement which rendered the country unknown, and the want of roads, which rendered it inaccessible. Then, till now the people have been almost exclusively employed in the fishing industries. The fisherman never saw farther than his own nose, and to him the plough that was known to old father Adam was an awkward and un-

THE TENTH ISLAND 145

familiar implement. Small wonder, then, that the progress of agriculture has been slow. Yet, despite these drawbacks, it is wonderful to see how quickly the fisherman is turning his new lesson to account. As yet the cultivation of land is confined to the vicinity of the towns and settlements, with two exceptions in the Humber River region, where a man named Nicholls has a farm, and where two sons of a clergyman, one of them formerly secretary to the Governor, have gone out to clear the land and to try their fortunes.

According to the latest census, there are 179,215 acres of land occupied, 64,494 acres of improved land, 20,524 acres in pasture, 21,813 acres in gardens, and 6,244 acres of improved land unused. I have seen it estimated that, at 50 dols. an acre (which land so close to towns is certainly worth), the territory at present cultivated is worth 3,224,700 dols. In 1884 the quantity of improved land was 46,498 acres; in 1900 I shall be astonished if it be less than 150,000 acres.

To show what a profitable business farming in Newfoundland can be made to be is to show how inconceivably stupid are the inhabitants, and how inconceivably foolish and ignorant are those persons who push forward to prosecute stock and crop-raising farther west, even to the heart of the continent. The prices

K

that ordinary produce fetches in St John's ought to have tempted experienced farmers to engage in this territory. The total value of the farm produce of the colony, I am informed, is 1,502,398 dols.; and every year a million dollars is spent on imported farm products. The colony, which could produce as good as Canada, spends an item of a quarter of a million dollars on butter and cheese alone. This would be all very well if it were a rich colony or unable to yield enough for its own consumption; but for a poor struggling community, which needs every dollar it can get and keep, and has besides such a belt of grazing country as I have never seen surpassed for richness, it is the purest extravagance. Of course, such things as making a stupid people sensible or a poor country prosperous are not to be done in the turning of a wrist; yet I cannot but think that a very few measures and a very few years would be required to so alter the face of this island and the conditions of life which govern it, that poor rusty, moping Cinderella would not know herself for the transformation. There are thousands upon thousands of acres of alfalfa grass, which might support thousands of cattle all the year round, for it cures itself on the stalk; and yet there is not even an old broken-down donkey to feast upon it.

While I was in the Humber River region I

had a most interesting talk with Mr Bayly, the elder of the two brothers I have mentioned. He told me they had begun business almost without a pound of capital, clearing the land with their own hands at the rate of twelve acres a year; and that they were succeeding even beyond their expectations. They found a capital market for everything they could raise; and, as we chatted, the ruddy hue of my gentleman-farmer's cheek, and the sparkle of his eye, made me envy his enthusiasm. Next year they would double the amount of their clearing, and build a couple of new outhouses, and buy more poultry. They could have a thousand more acres for a song, if they wanted it.

The alfalfa seed recently sown on his farm had proved thoroughly successful. It had withstood the storms and frosts of winter, and he expected to sow a great deal next year. Alfalfa grass, for stock-raising purposes, promises to prove invaluable.

A cosier farm already I could scarce wish to see: everything—to the farmhouse—the work of their own hands, and every penny of profit continually adding to the store. This is the sort of Swiss Family Robinson life which makes the heart-sick literary drudge want to start at once to be a farmer in a new country, unrestricted by landlords, untaxed by tithes, and uncoddled by curates. I have scarce a single pictorial souvenir which I treasure more than the two photographs which I carried away of the Bayly farm, with its plucky young proprietors, smiling and erect, in the middle distance.

All along the river flats, in the valleys, and on the "barrens," when these are subjected to drainage, and the country becomes cleared, there will be room for thousands of farms. The hills will furnish pasture for countless herds of cattle and sheep; and I hear there is already talk of starting ranches in this region. My own belief, based on observations in the ranching country of the North-West, is that such a business would pay handsomely. Cattle thus raised could be transported in five or six days to England, and would arrive in the pink of condition, instead of jaded by weeks of overland and sea travel. Thus, again, the proximity to England of such ranches as these figures greatly. To show how productive the soil is in the vicinity of St George's Bay, one has only to mention a fact which I learned there, that whenever the trees are removed by fire, wind, or other causes, a spontaneous growth of grass springs up. I was told of a vast meadow which has been giving hay for nineteen years, the nineteenth crop better than the first. With the adoption of the cold storage system, there are no limits to the success which might attend the prosecution of

THE TENTH ISLAND

the cattle and meat trade in Newfoundland. The freezing process could be very readily put into operation.

From the Humber River district to Hall's Bay, an arm of Notre Dame Bay, on the north-eastern coast, a level plain extends across the island. I believe the greatest height of land between these two points does not exceed 200 feet, and the distance is approximately 100 miles. In this plain the land is in many places almost equally excellent, and the timber abundant and of large size. At one time it was intended to construct a common road along this plain, and a survey was made some years ago, but no road ever came of it. From the surveyor's report, it appears that from 5000 to 8000 people could settle here with every prospect of making comfortable homes for themselves as farmers, lumbermen, or miners. A chain of small lakes, with rivers flowing from them, extends from Hall's Bay to the shores of Grand Lake, with only a single portage a mile in width. From Grand Lake the route lies across a portage nine miles wide, and then the Humber River is reached. The scenery along this plain, especially at the Birchy Ponds, is very beautiful, and several places compare not unfavourably with the lake scenery of England and Scotland. Game of various kinds is profuse, and great herds of deer are common sights.

Sportsmen may pardonably reckon this country

a paradise. It is said that nearly one thousand caribou were slaughtered about Gander Lake when swimming across in November 1893—truly a wanton and barbarous destruction. As to other game, the North American hare is found in prodigious numbers, and ptarmigan are plentiful. The beaver and other fur-bearing animals, bears, and wolves are met with. The island offers some of the finest grouse-shooting in America (the best localities being in the southern parts), and wild geese, ducks, snipe, and curlew are abundant.

As to the fisherman, the Tenth Island offers him unrivalled attractions. The lakes and rivers teem with trout and salmon.

Indian Brook Valley contains 50 square miles of land suitable for farming, and the timber area is not less than 100 square miles. The timber is chiefly white pine, white and black spruce, white birch, and fir. The soil is of a rich, sandy loam, easily worked.

As to what might be described as the centre of the island, I can bear even stronger personal testimony. The fertility of the lower Exploits Valley is amply testified wherever cultivation has ever been, even in the slightest degree, attempted; while as a grazing or stock-raising country it can hardly be surpassed. With a splendid river, plenteous timber, and a fertile soil, the region that is now a wilderness might, by energy and enterprise, be soon converted into a thriving settlement, maintaining a large population.

As regards Avalon, most of that peninsula consists of poor, rocky, swampy, or absolutely barren soil. I should not be disposed to think much of the possibilities of this part of the island, or rather of this which is almost an island by itself, if I had not seen equally poor land elsewhere converted by the virtues of the plough and manure into good oat, barley, and root crop lands. And what can be done in Scotland and New England can be done in Avalon. The gardens and cultivated areas in the neighbourhood of nearly all the settlements there bear witness to its possibilities, and already its rather thin soil furnishes admirable grazing ground, and extensive areas are already in the vicinity of the railway being turned to highly profitable account.

When you speak of farming, climate counts for a good deal. I was told that the Anglo-American Cable Company's shares were once called, in stock-exchange parlance, "dogs"; and I hear there is a tendency to speak of the new Newfoundland bond issue, in the same quarter, as "fogs." The French sage has observed that those evil qualities we most reprehend in others are those which most characterise ourselves; and it is probably by the same token that a travelling Cockney will stand anything sooner than a fog. Permeated to the primal artery by his "pea-soup," gasping and choking for breath, unable to see your hand before your face, he will smile calmly and tell you it is "nothing." But if you seek to blast the fair conception he has formed of any territory under the sun, tell him it is rather foggy, and you have settled its chance, so far as he is concerned, almost as much as if you had brought about its complete submersion by the sea.

Those early merchant-adventurers, with their fund of fog yarns, well knew what they were about.

Instead of the cold, foggy atmosphere which is generally supposed to hang over the island, the case is quite the reverse. The air is clear and warm, and the temperature during the year singularly equable, the mercury in winter seldom falling below zero or rising above 80 degrees in summer. If fogs visit the south-east and south-west corners of the island, as I am told they occasionally do, I never saw a shadow of one. At any rate, they never penetrate the interior, and I am ready to take it on the word of a clergyman who has spent many years here, that from June to October the climate is far superior to that of Great Britain, while the winters are many degrees milder than those of Nova Scotia or

New Brunswick, to say nothing of Minnesota and Manitoba.

On the whole, I think we may regard the fog bogey as played out. He has had his day—and a long day it has been. Let us be charitable: let us place him on the shelf.

CHAPTER XIV

It is not in the sea that the Tenth Island's biggest treasure lies. Nor is it on the land: it is under it.

Newfoundland is, in a word, a treasure-house of minerals. Already she is the sixth copper-producing country of the world. Yet, of copper alone a tithe of the visible quantity has not been worked. The mines of Newfoundland, like almost everything else, are in their veriest infancy, and there is scarcely a peasant who cannot show you on his mantel-shelf a specimen of the copper, iron, nickel, and even gold ore of his neighbourhood.

Various mines of asbestos, nickel, iron pyrites, lead, and iron in different parts of the island are already reckoned as actual property; and give promise of becoming, when the time arrives to work them properly, developments of great value.

Geological science has, I believe, long pointed to Newfoundland as being rich in mineral formations; but I was, I confess, not a little astounded at the evidence of this which, not only in my journeying in the interior, but in the capital and and on the coast, continually confronted me.

When in your rambles you discover the ground covered with shells or the soil strown with leaves you may make up your mind that ocean and wood are not far off; and when you are in a locality where every railway hand, fisherman, or lumberman, has not only got ore at home on his mantel-shelf, but carries seven kinds of it about in his trousers pocket, you may safely assure yourself you are in a mineral country. And that is what happens here. There is nothing so engrossing as the scientific mingled with the mysterious: which probably accounts for the seductions of astrology. But the astrological to the rude minds of those of whom I speak pales before the potency of a piece of rock or quartz which may or may not be worth millions. When I arrived in the colony the Cape Broyle gold fever had just reached its climax. Everybody who could rake and scrape enough together to reach that more or less favoured spot had staked off his or her little claim, never dreaming in their innocence of the pains of prospecting, of the weary labour of ledging, of the costs of mining plants, even of the humble stamping mill, to say nothing of capital-hunting, company-floating, and of that hope deferred, so common with miners, which maketh the heart sick. On the contrary, each individual seemed to regard the best part of the business done, now that he had staked his claim.

"What do you think of that, sir?" asked one man of me at the City Club, passing over to me for my inspection a fragment of clay-coloured ore about the size of a hen's egg. There was a look of triumph about his face, as who should say, I am not asking you for your praise but for your congratulation. I took the piece of ore, admiring the thin yellow vein which ran through its surface.

"What is the assayer's opinion?" I asked.

"I haven't shown to any assayer," he replied; "but there ain't any doubt about its being gold. You see I took it down here to a jeweller in Water Street, and he touched it up with acid. It's genuine gold right enough."

"What are you going to do with it?" I enquired.

"Sell it—if I can get my figure."

"Do you think there is much ore of this character on your claim?" His look answered my question. "And what do you regard as a reasonable price for the property?"

"Fifty thousand dollars," he replied promptly.

"But you won't get anybody to buy it at that figure until you've got expert opinion, sunk a shaft, and got the ore properly assayed."

"Very well; then I won't sell it. The gold's there all right; it can't walk away, and when I get ready, I'll do all these things myself."

When I came to make further inquiries about the Cape Broyle discoveries, I found that the gold seam, although fairly rich, was of paltry extent. By the time, therefore, that it reached this man's claim, it had probably nearly petered out altogether. As a proof of this, I was afterwards told that, although the territory had been dug up in all directions, a few pounds of ore worth 7 dols., was all that rewarded the mine-owner in prospective, who would not part with his claim under 50,000 dols. Since then, many of the Cape Broyle claims have been abandoned.

But that there is gold elsewhere cannot be doubted.

The abnormal development of the serpentine rocks in the island, is regarded by geologists as sustaining their assertion that Newfoundland is a remarkable mineral country. The shores of Notre Dame Bay, where copper was first unearthed, are of serpentine formation, as well as its many clusters of islands. At Bay of Islands and Bonne Bay, on the west coast, there are large developments of the serpentine; and I am told there are reasons for believing that the serpentine formation traverses the island between these two points. The existence of the new railway will greatly facilitate the exploration of this region, and then a true knowledge of the extent of its mineral deposits will ultimately be revealed.

As to the actual copper wealth of the island, the first mine was discovered in 1857 at a small fishing hamlet known as Tilt Cove. The discovery was soon turned into an enterprise, and the enterprise into a profit. In the course of fifteen years the Tilt Cove mine yielded somewhere about 50,000 tons of copper ore, worth 1,572,154 dols.; as well as 32,740 dols. worth of nickel ore. It is still worked at the present day, giving employment to several hundred miners. Eighteen years after the discovery of Tilt Cove, another copper mine was opened at Bett's Cove, a dozen miles to the south; and in 1878 an even richer copper deposit was unearthed at Little Bay. Up to 1879, the total value of the ores exported from these mines was close upon a million pounds sterling.

The present mineral exports approximated a million dollars annually. But I believe there has been of late years a very serious slump in copper—owing to the enormous output in the Lake Superior mines, and the determination of those controlling those properties to under-sell all possible rivals. Nevertheless, the demand grows yearly greater as the result of modern electrical contrivances, and prices are slowly advancing. When they reach that point, a few dollars more a ton, which they are confidently expected soon to reach, there is no doubt about capital's intentions in the matter. It is the opinion of American experts that no finer copper than that in Newfoundland can be found. That in the Tilt Cove mine is a beautiful yellow sulphuret, free from arsenic or any undesirable ingredient, with a little iron, and containing from eight to twelve per cent. of pure copper. According to an American expert, Professor Stewart, the "character of the rocks in which copper occurs gives an absolute assurance of perpetuity in the working. The rocks are metamorphosed and laminated; and the extent of mineral indications over large areas renders exhaustion in the working a practical impossibility."

After this, Newfoundland should feel easy about her copper supply.

Passing from copper to other ores, Mr Howley, the head of the Geological Survey, informs me that iron, lead, coal, asbestos, manganese, antimonite, molybdenite, and silver, as well as gold, occur in various places, and frequently in promising quantities. Lead ore was first discovered at La Manche, near the north-eastern extremity of Placentia Bay, where workings were carried on for several years. The quality of the lead was of the best, with a slight percentage of silver. At Port-au-Port, on the western shore of the island, a rich deposit of lead ore was discovered some years ago, and for a short time was worked with most favourable results. On the protest of the French, however, who alleged that the working of a mine here was an infringement of their treaty rights, the Imperial authorities ordered a cessation of the enterprise. This was not the first, nor has it been the last, occasion on which a similar episode has occurred.*

In St George's Bay and Codroy the developments of gypsum are enormous, but, after copper and iron, it is in coal and asbestos that the island is richest. The deposit of the latter mineral has attracted the most attention on account of its great scarcity in America, and the not distant prospect of the Canadian supply giving out. Prospectors were sent to the island in great numbers; for asbestos is an article not to be found in every acre. It is a little singular that a mineral substance which can be utilised for the manufacture of clothing, and even of lace curtains, is the only substance which will effectually close the breach of a 110-pound gun so as to prevent the escape of gas when the charge is fired, for covering war-balloons, and for protecting the sides of iron-

---

* In the Appendix is set forth the case of Captain Cunningham, whose mining operations were terminated at the instance of the French.

clads. The quality of the asbestos found is highly satisfactory. The way it came to be found at all is curious. On the eastern coast of Port-au-Port, rising out of the sea to a nearly vertical height of 1800 feet, is a mountain known as Bluff Head. This mountain was long known to the fishermen of the locality as "Cotton Rock," on account of the fibrous character of the stone thereabouts. The "cotton" was long collected in small quantities, and shown among the men, their wives and children, as a curiosity. The tale and the "cotton" passed from fisherman to fisherman, until a morsel of both got into the hands of a St John's legislator, who pricked up his ears and opened his eyes and declared the stuff was asbestos. Whereupon he equipped a small expedition, who went prospecting, finding fibre five inches long, of beautiful silky texture. Then began the asbestos boom. I have mentioned the advent of prospectors and exports. One of them, who came out from England, shows why, even more than from diplomatic causes, mining on the west coast is no child's play.

"If we had only a cattle track to pass over," he said, "it would be something. I have found asbestos and wish to open a mine; but to do this I have to encounter extraordinary difficulties. When I reach the gravels at Port-au-Port I have about twelve miles to go; but the country there is in a primeval state. There is no road or path or even cattle track; consequently we must go by water. All our goods, too, must go by water, and the products of the mines must go the same way. The coast line here is rugged in the extreme, and by water, I believe, the distance is about fifteen miles. Now, so great is the difficulty of this passage, occasioned by the cross currents and sudden squalls passing over the crest of the hills, that I have frequently been kept out for twelve hours during the trip. The landing on the rock is, from the state of the surf on the rocky coast, always more or less in the nature of a shipwreck. Twice I have had my davy smashed up, and twice the men were wrecked, and on one occasion I was detained on this inhospitable coast for three mortal days before we could launch a boat to get off. Such a state of things is discreditable to the country, and nothing, I believe, can be found like it in any other part of the civilised world."

But the new railway will soon put a stop to all this. That the country has not long ere this taken a first rank as a mineral producer is, of course, the result of its former isolated position, difficulty of access, except in small sailing vessels, and other ulterior causes. Now, however, with regular and frequent steam communication, the prospector and the engineer are gradually forcing their way into the country, which seems destined to be the scene of prosperous mining camps, and a profitable mining industry.

Mr Howley's predecessor in the Geological Survey, after a most careful exploration of the St George's Bay region, calculated that the plan of a single coal seam, 3 feet thick, and occupying an area of 38 square miles, contains 54,720,000 chaldrons of coal. To-day the principal discovered seams are 4 feet, 3½, and 1½ feet thick, and experts have calculated that if shipments of 250,000 tons a year were made, it would take a century to exhaust the coal beds of St George's Bay alone. The Cape Ray discoveries last year are believed to surpass any coal deposits yet found. It is a very bituminous caking coal, emitting much gas under combustion, and burning freely. Yet, so far from any of the discovered seams being worked, the importation of coal, mainly from Cape Breton, amounts to more than 100,000 tons annually. If the coal mines in St George's Bay worked, why should not the whole of this consumption be supplied from these local deposits? Apparently there is no reason why it should not; and I venture to predict that in a year or two this will be done, as a preliminary to the shipment of coal from one of the greatest coal-fields on earth. The money now sent out of the country will be employed in paying the wages of miners, and in carrying on mining operations, and a great impulse given thereby to trade in all its ramifications.

I was shown by several persons, among them Governor Murray, samples of the oil of this district, and although I profess to know nothing whatever as to its quality, yet the testimony of experts is that it is equal in every respect to the Pennsylvania and Ohio product. Two or three companies have already been started to work the new petroleum finds; and I am told that not only have the owners every faith in them, but that several of the properties would command to-morrow very high prices. To show the faith of capital in the mineral resources of Newfoundland, I may here mention that several of the enterprises have already changed hands for figures the reverse of low. For example, the iron pyrites mine on Pilley's Island was bought for 300,000 dols. by Yankee capitalists, and they have since refused a much higher price. In 1893, this mine alone sent 195,780 dols. worth of ore to the States; which is certainly on the face of it no mean return for such an investment.

The Novia Scotia Steel Company has been working for two years the vast — indeed, practically inexhaustible—deposits of hematite on Bell Isle in Conception Bay. Three hundred men are employed there all the time, and there is a good market in New Glasgow and Baltimore. Then, again, when I left Newfoundland there were several parties out from Workington, in Cumberland, representing an English syndicate formed to operate in hematite. At Baie de Verde the deposit is fourteen miles long, and a lease has been signed for a yearly rental at £2800 sterling, royalty at 3d. per ton. The same strata runs along the north shore of Conception Bay, and, indeed, the whole country-side is believed to be a mine of hematite close to the water, with unequalled shipping facilities, cheap labour, and no mechanical and other difficulties in the way of its development.

Along the line of the railway through the island immense deposits of coal have been struck—one at Grand Lake and the other at Codroy. The latter is of singular economic value, for it is close to the sea and within thirty miles of Port-aux-Basques. This coal is expected to compete with the Sydney coal in supplying ships plying up and down the St Lawrence, for every such ship goes within sight of Channel or Port-aux-Basques, which, as I have said, is the terminus of the railway, whereas for the ships to get coal at Sydney means a deviation of ninety miles from their direct track.

Her Majesty's ships now import Welsh coal, because they say that Nova Scotian coal blackens their paint, but Mr Howley thinks that the warships will in time avail themselves of the Newfoundland deposits. I have mentioned the arguments in favour of making St John's a British naval station.

On the west coast, again, there is a big mine of chrome iron, which is used largely in making chrome steel for warships.

Marbles of almost every colour have been produced from various sections of the coast, the development at Bay of Islands being perhaps most extensive. In addition to this, granite of the finest quality, building stone, limestone, and slate are famed in abundance.

Newfoundland is all ready for the prospector and working miner. Cinderella seems to have guarded herself against being taken unawares. She has, in effect, framed laws and enactments covering this ground.

When any person shall discover a vein, lode, or deposit of mineral, and seeks to obtain a lease, he is bound to mark the land by four boundary posts or cairns. The extent of enclosed land must not exceed one square mile, and the claim-owner is obliged, as soon as possible, to apply to the Surveyor-General for a licence, and deposit a fee of 20 dols.: the first notice filed to give priority of claim. The first licence shall be for a year; a payment of 30 dols. shall entitle to a licence for another year, and a farther sum of 50 dols. to an extension for another year. During the second year the licensee must expend the sum of 200 dols., or its equivalent in labour, in exploring and developing minerals in the said mining location. If his faith holds out for a third year he must spend 400 dols. or else relinquish the claim to somebody else. According to the law, at any time during a continuance of the licence or its renewals, the licensee may apply for a lease of the location, depositing with the Surveyor-General the sum of 50 dols., when the Governor in Council may issue a mining lease and a lease of fifty acres of unoccupied surface land within such mining location for the term of five years from the date of application therefor. Only such lease shall be subject to the condition that the lessee shall expend in and about the working of such mines and minerals, during each of the first four years from the date of the lease, the sum of 800 dols., and during the fifth year 2800 dols.

Other clauses of the mining enactments of the colony provide that licences of search for gold over an area not exceeding one-half square mile may be issued for a period of one year on payment of a fee of 25 dols., renewable for another year on payment of a fee of 50 dols. Leases to mine and work gold, over an area not exceeding one quarter of a square mile, may be issued for a period of twenty-one years subject to a royalty of three per cent. on the gold mined. This is not without interest in view of the enactments in connection with the recent discoveries of gold elsewhere.

Altogether, the possession of so many useful minerals and economic substances as I have enumerated in a territory so near to Europe, should point to Newfoundland as a country most favourably equipped for mining and manufacturing. In its mineral wealth, I doubt if it stands second to any British-American possession; but its not least powerful recommendation is that labour is both abundant and cheap. Thousands of fishermen are as ready to grapple for wealth in the bowels of the earth as they are to perform the same operation within the bosom of the vasty deep.

CHAPTER XV

I HAVE dwelt—in a somewhat hasty and desultory fashion—on the salient features of Newfoundland. I have seen and interviewed the people who rule the island, and those who live in it. I now propose to speak of the man who owns it.

Not, be it understood, all of it. That, under the peculiar political circumstances, would soon perhaps constitute a kingship, even as Mr Harden-Hickey became le Roi de Trinidad. But 5000 acres would be a goodly possession in Ireland. Mr Robert Reid possesses 5000 square miles in Newfoundland. This gentleman is, therefore, merely the grand duke of the island.

It was Mr Reid who undertook to build and operate the Newfoundland Railway. To thoroughly appreciate the nature of this great exploit, one should remember that building a railway in Newfoundland is not exactly the same thing as constructing them elsewhere. Only such as have organised an operation like railway building through a wild country can appreciate all the difficulties that must be faced: the organisation—of raw material, unskilled labour—required, the toil and foresight necessary to provide food and shelter for a small army of workmen, the precautions against accidents, disaffection, lack of supplies and working material — all of which is incidental to the construction of a railway in a new country. It was only twenty years ago that the man who even spoke in favourable fashion of a railway in Newfoundland ran some risk of bodily injury.

It was only fifteen years ago that the inhabitants of the south shore of Conception Bay, believing all the terrible tales that were told them about that monster, the railway, stoned the engineers, took away their instruments, and drove them from their work. The inspector of police and the police magistrate, with only eleven men, were left to battle with a frenzied mob of 500 people of both sexes, armed with sealing-guns, stones, and bludgeons. The very name railway suggested to the fisher-folk a mighty ogre—cruel, relentless, forbidding — a term wherewith to half-scare the senses out of intractable children. If the reader smile, incredulous, he has merely to recall the precisely similar attitude of the English peasant toward the steam-engine less than a century ago. For five days the whole population from Topsail to Indian Pond were in an insane state of excitement. Though it was the busiest time of the year, they never did a stroke of work; all day they watched the engineers and the small posse of police, and followed them from place to place. They truly believed that "the advent of this terrible monster, the railway, meant their ruin."*

But the first railway was got under weigh: and at the close of the working season twenty miles were graded and ten miles metalled.

By this time the fishermen began to look upon the railway in a different light. Caliban was growing tamer. Although he could not for the life of him understand it, he was being paid handsomely to fell trees, to shovel earth, and to load and unload sleepers. Indeed, he was paid so handsomely that the company which had undertaken to build the railway went into liquidation long before the line was even one-half completed. I heard some of the most amusing stories of the fishermen in connection with this first railway experience of the colony; and one can readily believe the process of knocking together a railway to have been highly humorous for all except the contractors.

But the colony was not to be baulked of her line. Little by little the inhabitants began to catch the railway fever—perhaps one of the

---

* Prowse's "History of Newfoundland."

most virulent of all known infections. From loathing and dreading the railway, they began to admire and embrace it; and soon every legislator in the island was pledged to get a Bill passed for a railway of some sort beginning somewhere and ending somewhere else in his district. Rough-looking citizens began pouring into the capital from the outports, to make inquiries as to why no more railways were being built. At last, the Government, dreading unpopularity, and finding no more contractors ready to build railways, determined to construct a line—a very limited one—on its own account. I may mention on authority, that although anywhere would have answered the purpose, the particular line to Placentia was resolved upon to obtain the political adhesion of the two members for that district, and that it took two years to complete, and cost 750,000 dols.

It only remains for me to add that the new railway boasted the inordinate length of 27 miles.

No wonder the fishermen grinned and rubbed their hands! No wonder the more sensible taxpayers of the colony, who had long been advocating railways, began to look aghast at the proceedings. More railway measures were passed; and in 1889 the Government decided to resume the building of the railway to Hall's Bay, which the defunct company had left two-thirds uncompleted. But when ten or fifteen miles had been built, in a most dilettante and rambling manner, a new Government came into power, and a new man came upon the scene.

This person, whom I hope I do not libel in referring to as the largest private landowner in the world, was a Montreal railway contractor. In his office in the Canadian metropolis he had been seated one day, with a map of North America hung before him on the wall. He had already amassed a large fortune, and could look back on a long and adventurous career. As a penniless Scotch lad, he had left his home and gone to seek his fortune in Australia, where ability and shrewdness pushed him along, and prosperity came to him wherever he went. He at length migrated to Canada, and, in the capacity of contractor, built large portions of the Canadian Pacific Railway. He was now a wealthy man, a thorough master of his business, and, although somewhat enfeebled in health, already looking out for new fields of endeavour. As he contemplated the map, he was immediately struck by the geographical situation of Newfoundland. He remembered the vague reports he had heard of the colony, and he made a X in blue pencil on the map.

"That," he remarked quietly to a friend, "is the coming country."

A short time elapsed and the news reached Mr Reid that Newfoundland wanted somebody to build the island a railway. The colony was advertising for tenders. In the tender he despatched to the Government he offered to build the road at 15,000 dols. a mile. The offer was accepted. Upon the heels of this acceptance the colony was astonished by the celerity with which the new contractor got to work. Mr Reid's faith in the colony was greater than the Government's. The latter had only considered a railway to Hall's Bay, the former was ready, not only to build it across the island, and take their bonds in exchange at a time when Newfoundland bonds—technically know as "Fogs"—were at a low ebb, but also something more. A railway is a useless concern if it be unoperated. Mr Reid offered, then, to operate the new railway.

The cost of operation was estimated at £20,000 sterling annually.

The Government then agreed to "grant in fee-simple to the contractor 5000 acres of land for each one mile of main line or branch railway throughout the entire length of line to be operated," in respect of its operation for ten years. Also, in addition, to pay 60,000 dols. a year by way of a mails subsidy.

When the news of this arrangement became public, not a little indignation prevailed among a large class of respectable persons in the capital. They felt that Mr Reid had been imposed upon.

One gentleman overwhelmed the new contractor with his condolences.

"I'm really very sorry this thing has happened," he said. "Why didn't you come to me? I could have told you all this land wasn't worth a d—d red cent."

The millionaire smiled inscrutably. He is still smiling; his descendants will go on smiling even unto the third and fourth generation. Mr Reid is not a young man, but he has associated with him three clever stalwart sons, who promise to be among the wealthiest and most powerful men in the world.

From the moment the first sod was cut they became Newfoundlanders. They did not delegate the work to others, but went at it tooth and nail, toiling with the men, sharing their fare and hardships, and even their personal risks. And now the last sod is cut, the last spike driven, and the Newfoundland railway is finished. I was talking with a man who said to me, I know not by what authority:

"Reid has built a first-class road; but his profits will be at least half a million sterling. In other words, the profits and the subsidy will more than operate the line, and he has got 2,500,000 acres, much of it rich timber, agricultural, and mineral land, into the bargain."

Supposing that to be true, and I will not vouch that it is, how many millionaires would have approached such a project with a pair of tongs? To take its bonds and its lands in payment required more confidence in the colony than any other man has ever shown since it was discovered by Cabot. If, indeed, Robert Reid's Newfoundland land and railway monopoly turns out as great and greater as Robert Dunsmuir's monopoly of Vancouver Island, I can only say that what was in one case due, in the first instance, to pure luck, is due here to hard work and foresight. The policy of the Dunsmuir family has been to retard the progress of their great island as much as possible; that of the Reids will be to advance theirs. To encourage settlement will be the great aim and object. I do not think a Scotchman like Mr Reid ever dreams of the picturesque side of his position. The idea of erecting a baronial castle on his vast domain and inviting over brother princes to a house-warming has probably never entered his head. It has several times entered mine: it is rather a fascinating notion — the largest landowner on earth!

While his surveyors are at present laying off the iron, coal, and oil territory, Mr Reid himself is away in Europe seeing the fine new steamer built that is to carry his passengers across the gulf to the Canadian shore. That no time is being lost is apparent.

One of the immediate results of the new rail-

THE TENTH ISLAND 177

way has been the opening up of common roads to connect settlement with settlement, and thereby feed the line. These roads have mostly been surveyed and built by the contractor, acting under instructions from Government, and new life imparted to lonely, isolated settlements thus placed in easy communication with the capital.

To the sportsman, the tourist, the angler, and the canoeist, the new railway will offer unrivalled attractions. It will bring him right upon the deer park at Grand Lake, a body of water fifty miles long, down which he may proceed by boat and place his camp.

The development of a fast transatlantic service will depend on the development of the island. But I have no doubt it will come—in time.

The honour of first suggesting this project of a fast line belongs to Mr Sandford Fleming, C.B. Mr Fleming's original proposal was to run a line of steamers, built expressly for speed, between St John's, Newfoundland, and Valentia, Ireland.

The distance between these two ports is but little more than half the distance between Liverpool and New York.

But it is now seen by the advocates of the fast line that, owing to the present construction of the railway, steamers should choose a more northerly port than St John's, say Bonavista Bay, and also in order to escape the fogs. At Bona-

M

vista the steamer would be met by an express train, which would whirl them over the island at the rate of fifty miles an hour. Thus not only the shortest ocean passage would be secured, but the discomforts attendant on crossing the Atlantic would be so diminished that it would have no more terrors for passengers than a voyage across the Irish Channel, and the list of casualties would be vastly lessened.

All the dangers of the voyage lie along the American coast, between Cape Race and New York, where thick fogs and treacherous currents prevail, and where nearly all wrecks of steamers have occurred. The late Mr Thomas Cook once gave me his estimate that there were in Great Britain a million "potential" Atlantic voyagers. Compare this with the actual 50,000. Who would encounter the perils of rocks, shoals, fogs, and currents, and, above all, the protracted discomforts of sea-sickness, when he could shoot across the Atlantic in three and a half days (or less) to Newfoundland; then be whisked in eight hours in a cosy Pullman to Port-aux-Basque, and three hours later find himself on the continent of America, whirling towards Montreal, New York, or Chicago, in the rear of the iron steed?

I found many in Newfoundland sceptical about the gold discoveries—even Mr Howley, F.R.G.S., the Government geologist. I found many shake their heads over the fast line scheme. But there was no mistaking which commanded most their enthusiasm. If I had interviewed John Wesley as to his chances of Paradise, he, too, fearful of offending Providence, would doubtless have shaken his head.

"Looking over the situation calmly," said a Newfoundlander to me, "it does not seem to me creditable to modern enterprise that so great an opportunity should have been so long neglected, or that this island which lies nearest to Britain's shores, should not form part of the route between Britain and the Far West."

Professor Huxley once said that "if the sea were drained off you might drive a waggon from Valentia, Ireland, to Trinity Bay, Newfoundland." He was describing the prodigious plain—one of the widest and most even plains in the world—which is known to exist under the sea, as well as if it were visible, between those points. Along this plain the first cables were laid. Over it the fast steamers ought to run.

CHAPTER XVI

When a French smuggler has a particularly bright dream—he dreams that he has gone to St Pierre.

St Pierre is not a part of our Empire—that is owing to the blessed maladroitness of our Foreign Office — but it is his whole North American empire to the Frenchman. This busy but barren little island — for I need scarcely mention Miquelon, which is but as the tail of the dog to the dog itself, is all that remains to him of his once proud dominions—Canada, the Mississippi and Ohio valleys, and Louisiana. And there, I may add, to-day the insignificant little terrier barks and yelps, while the poor old cow looks mildly on, whom nobody, certainly not the French tax-payer, would blame were it to lower its horns and toss the futile little beast into the centre of the Arctic Archipelago.

St Pierre at present forms a basis for three distinct operations—

1. The French Bank and treaty shore fisheries.
2. Diplomatic intrigue.
3. Smuggling.

I have endeavoured in previous pages to set forth the two systems of Bait-procuring and

Bounty-giving, but for which systems—the latter built on childish and wicked fallacy, but sedulously fostered by the French Government—St Pierre and Miquelon would cease to be. The whole French transatlantic fishery is a structure resting on two frail pillars. One of these pillars is Bounty, and the other is Bait.

There are probably not more than 2500 *bonâ fide* Frenchmen despatched to the Newfoundland cod-fishery. Over and above the value of their catch, they cost the French Treasury from three to five million francs—a small sum, but a sum utterly and needlessly thrown away. It serves no good end: the sugar bounties at least foster the culture of beetroot. Remove the sugar bounties and beetroot might possibly stand on its legs along with sugar-cane; repeal the cod-fish bounties and the cod-fish would be no nearer French coasts than ever, or the coasts of its dependencies.

Not only is the prosperity of St Pierre fictitious, its acts nefarious, its position illogical, but its very existence is illegal.

By what singular mischance was the orginal treaty overlooked, by which these islands were generously ceded to France, when the first violation of that treaty took place? They were given over by the Treaty of Paris, 1763, to serve as a "shelter to French fishermen," and a solemn stipulation was exacted that no buildings were to be erected " but merely for the convenience of the fishery" and "to keep a guard of fifty men only for the police." There were to be no permanent dwellings, no fixed population, certainly no fortifications, no Governor, no Hotel de Ville, no custom-house, no newspapers—in a word, no colony. It was to be simply a convenience—a temporary refuge for the fishermen sent out from France, and nothing more.

To state the case simply, the French have illicitly erected a flourishing colony in our own waters which our Government does not recognise as a colony, and to which no consul or agent of ours is accredited, but which, though the two islands together are scarce bigger than the Isle of Wight, is the basis for commercial and political intrigue, whereby *our* neighbouring colonies are enormously injured. St Pierre is one vast smuggling hive. It has warehouses stocked with cases of wines, spirits, tea, and tobacco ready for nefarious shipment to the adjacent coasts of Canada, Newfoundland, and the United States. I heard it passed openly from mouth to mouth that the American Consul was at the head of the illicit trade with the States. This is sadly irregular; but, at all events, that is something, and my Consular friend's profits must be enormous. But I think it only fair that, if our fellow-countrymen of Canada and the Tenth Island are to be robbed, they should at least be robbed by one of themselves. It is a shame that it should be all done by a Frenchman, especially as the post is such a lucrative one.

I only wish the Foreign Office would appoint me Consul-General to St Pierre; and from thence, I am assured, it would be but a step to Park Lane.

And what is the charm of St Pierre and the fishery to the Frenchman—the Frenchman of France—the poor tax-payer who is asked every year to contribute millions of francs to keep up this beggarly little colony in North America? He is told by his Government, and the Quai d'Orsay tells ours, that St Pierre and the fishery is dear to France because it is the nursery of the navy. Our Government accepts the explanation; but do you think the intelligent Frenchman believes for a moment that such is the case. Not he. I have lived—*moi qui parle*—in France, and I have talked with Frenchmen at home as well as abroad, and I know that at the root and bottom of the French pertinacity in this matter is not that they may secure trained recruits for their navy (most of their men are sent thither in steamers, and every intelligent French naval officer recognises that the English system of training boys for the service is the only way to efficiently man your men-of-war), but sentiment—sentiment pure and simple. The Government that should propose to give up those two little islands, "the sole remnant of our once proud North American dominion," even were they ten times as expensive—as expensive, in fact, as Tonkin—would be instantly hooted from office. The Newfoundland French fishery, as a means of manning the navy, is a superannuated expedient. The Newfoundland fishery, as a means of keeping and colonising St Pierre and Miquelon, is worth to them all the money and pains this curiously sentimental people can expend upon it. So they will go on paying high bounties, and yet higher, on cod-fish; and soon, when the Newfoundland Government shows a firmer front, there will be a bounty on bait. It is not a mere question of commerce—no: *c'est l'honneur de la France!*

And now, having sufficiently discussed its significance, let me devote the rest of this chapter to St Pierre itself.

It is certainly a most picturesque little place—a tiny bit of old Brittany transplanted in the New World.

You see and hear, as one writer remarks, "the creaking ox-cart, the click of the sabot on the ill-constructed trottoir, the Breton, Basque, and apple-cheeked Norman women, the *patois*, the French windows, the gay colours, and, last of all, the fanfare of the bugle as the town-crier proclaims at each corner of the streets and squares,

THE TENTH ISLAND

after a preliminary blast of the trumpet, that M. Solomon will sell some "'bonne vaches a lait' at the Quai de la Roncière punctually to-morrow at ten o'clock."

The town lies on the east side of the island, and contains perhaps 6000 persons.

During the fishing season it presents a very busy aspect; its harbour, the only real harbour in the two islands, often contains hundreds of fishing vessels, besides dozens of mysterious craft which boast no fish; while thousands of grinning weather-beaten men are superadded to its population. The chief buildings are the Governor's House, where high revels are often held; the Court of Justice, a cathedral, convent and schools, the Treasury and Post Office buildings, Government provision store, and printing office. Some rather handsome private dwellings attract the eye—for why should not your bold buccaneer be well housed?—and there are hotels such as the Joinville, Pension Hacala, and the International House. Oh, decidedly the French have made the most of this island, $7\frac{1}{2}$ miles long, $5\frac{1}{2}$ miles wide, and 26 miles in circumference! There is, besides, a college, three schools taught by a brotherhood, and a girls' school taught by nuns — Sisters of the Order of St Joseph of Cluny — and a hospital.

To read the history of this droll little island, which we gave to the French in a moment of generosity, is to read a thing to make you laugh.* It is a Lilliputian reproduction of the contemporary history of France—the absurd toy-terrier imitating the lion. The little island had, like the Mother Country, its Revolution, its Reign of Terror, its Robespierre, its Committee of Public Safety, its bombastic philippics, its Jacobin Club, and, under the Empire, its microscopic *coup d'etat.* And all the tempest was in a teapot!

There is naturally plenty of money and plenty of hospitality in St Pierre—for the contraband trade is large and flourishing. In former years the imports of Newfoundland were about 36 dols. a head. The imports of St Pierre, on the other hand, I am informed, amount to over 480 dols., at least 450 dols. of which is smuggled into Newfoundland and Canada.

In peace or war, the old smuggling transactions have been carried on with scarce an interruption. The Pierrois, in this business, have plundered the revenues not only of Canada,

---

* It must be borne in mind that the colonies had then been for half-a-century the permanent home of a considerable English population. The Imperial Government was well acquainted with the immense value of St Pierre as a fishing station, and especially as headquarters for the Bank fishery. They were also well aware that its dangerous proximity to Newfoundland rendered it—as Lord Chatham declared—a constant menace to our Colony. Notwithstanding these facts, under this disgraceful treaty of 1763, the rights of the colonists and the property of the permanent English settlers at St Pierre were ruthlessly sacrificed.—PROWSE.

THE TENTH ISLAND

Newfoundland, and the States, but, if report be true, they have even found a way of robbing France of a greater sum than the island, with its Governor, its Court of Justice, its hotels, and its nuns and friars, and, indeed, everything but its "Government storehouse," would be bought for by any sensible nation in Europe. As the French pay a bounty nearly equal to the price of the fish, there is nothing to prevent your patriotic Pierrois from surreptitiously importing vast quantities of English-caught fish, receive the bounty, and dispose of the fish afterwards at a profit.

St Pierre is, besides, the centre of the bait trade. Each year, according to the French showing, the French fishermen pay 800,000 francs to the English fishermen for herring.

"Is this sum paid in cash?" I asked a well-to-do Pierrois.

"No!" he said, "not exactly in cash. You see, the English make considerable purchases in St Pierre. We are, *en effet*, nicely situated to collect the merchandise furnished both from France and America."

"And you, of course, facilitate the transfer, eh? sometimes on the high seas?"

The Frenchman grinned.

"We do—what you call it—meet your Newfoundlander half-way, maybe," he said.

All, or nearly all, these nice dark buildings

on the wharves, then, are stored with goods waiting for either clandestine shipment, which is stupid, or open shipment accompanied by false bills of lading and false clearances, which is clever.

When, years ago, one of Her Majesty's customs inspectors visited the island, he stated that Newfoundland revenue was robbed of enormous sums, and half the spirits and tobacco consumed in Lower Canada smuggled from the French colony.

St Pierre is practically a free port for tobacco, so that smuggling that article thence to Boston and Quebec, or more convenient ports on the Atlantic coast or shores of the St Lawrence, is now almost as profitable a business as the liquor traffic; spirituous liquors are admitted into St Pierre free of duty. I am told that a fleet of three-masted schooners is constantly kept going for the smugglers, carrying cargoes of alcohol from Boston to this port. Of course, there is no cause for concealment about this part of the traffic; the smuggling commences when the alcohol has to be landed at Canadian ports so as to avoid the duty of 2 dols. a gallon. There are two, and often three, transhipments of the liquor from the time it leaves the *entrepot* of St Pierre until it is safely put ashore upon the banks of the St Lawrence. All this is, as may be guessed, a very hardy and risky enterprise, especially as it is often conducted with small craft. The immense profit of the traffic may be estimated by the fact that the whisky or gin, which is the chief staple of the trade, sells for 1 dol. 40 cents a gallon in Boston, and is worth in Quebec no less than 3 dols. 75 cents. Jamaica rum, French liquours, and brandies, which are also admitted duty free into St Pierre, form a portion of most cargoes from St Pierre to Quebec and other ports.

The masters of the large gulf schooners leaving St Pierre with liquor aboard are shrewd enough not to risk a total loss of vessel and cargo by venturing so far as Canadian inland waters. Before leaving the mouth of the St Lawrence they are invariably met by three or four smaller craft, generally schooners of very small value, which divide among them the cargo of the larger craft. One of these may be seized and confiscated, and yet the profit upon the operations of the others will make the entire trip a lucrative one. Yet, if they are old hands at the business, they all manage to escape capture. Small boats again, in turn, land the liquor from the schooners, generally at night, at some of the parishes on the Isle of Orleans or elsewhere near Quebec.

Not a few of the parishes of the lower St

Lawrence have, according to one of their own newspapers, become completely demoralised by the proportions to which this traffic has grown. Many farmers neglect their land and fishermen their nets to engage in ventures which promise such large returns. The excitement and hardy life attendant upon it naturally offer great attractions to the French Canadian character.

Sometimes the smuggler shows fight—just as he does elsewhere. One noted smuggler, Captain Bouchard, fought, and compelled the retreat of a Government revenue cutter, and was only subdued and captured after he had been besieged in and dislodged from the smugglers' stronghold on the Isle-aux-Coudres, in the Lower St Lawrence. Verily there is a strong bond of brotherhood and sympathy between the French Canadian and the French St Pierrois! When the case of the worthy captain was tried, he was convicted of *simple assault*, and fined 25 dols.

I am not sure life is not more agreeably passed in St Pierre than it is in St John's; but so is life gayer in Lyons than in Liverpool. It is the French character. There are cafés—even cafés chantant — to drop into of an evening, and a general good-humouredness and odour of prosperity about.

In the old days the government was entrusted to a distinguished admiral. Even during the

Second Empire one finds the names of the genial Admiral Cloué and the Baron Ronciere le Noury. Nowadays these naval dignitaries are replaced by a lawyer from Paris, or a journalist from the provinces.

Altogether, I think I have made clear that St Pierre, although a very nice little fishing-town—far superior really to most fishing-towns—is very much in need of a British consul, or even an agent from that British colony which suffers so much from its existence. Several attempts have been made to fulfil this need; but a race of smugglers—although very delightful company, replete with racy anecdote and love of wassail—are not unnaturally impatient of men who come in the name of law and honesty. Wherefore I regret to say that each attempt to protect our interests in this island has been rudely repulsed, and our consul or agent unceremoniously kicked out. Looking to the peculiar grievances under which we suffer, the obvious retort to such informal proceedings as the foregoing would be to serve an ultimatum, and forthwith force our representative into easy quarters at the Hotel Joinville at the cannon's mouth, and accompanied by a muster of merry marines.

As it is, what do we do?

We grin. Our colony—the Tenth Island—bears it.

CHAPTER XVII

THE one really great problem which has confronted our Naval authorities for the past quarter of a century has been the adequate and efficient manning of the Fleet. It has struck many of those whose tastes, interests, or researches have led them in this direction as nothing short of a grave national danger that our Naval personnel not only does not keep pace with the other arm of the service, but is absurdly out of proportion to the growth of construction. The Admiralty, aided by a complaisant Chancellor of the Exchequer, and backed, perhaps, by the spirit of the nation, goes on building ships, for which, under present conditions, an efficient human equipment seems out of the question. For certain reasons, Naval recruits become each year more difficult to obtain. Perhaps the Navy has ceased to be as attractive to youth as formerly—perhaps the class from which recruits were in the old days wont to present themselves for enlistment has diminished—but the fact remains. The training-ships do not turn out a sufficient number of lads to meet requirements caused by death, disability, and discharge—or by the huge increase of battleships. It is only of a piece with the Englishman's innate conservatism that he has hitherto steadily refused, not merely to consider, but even to contemplate, what must strike an ordinary mind—let us say the mind of a foreigner—as a very obvious solution of the difficulty.

To increase the strength of the Navy, many propositions have been put forward. It is admitted that construction is going far ahead of personnel; but it is denied, in one quarter, that there would be any serious trouble in securing Naval recruits at home if the Admiralty chose to do so. It is asserted, and perhaps truly, that there is not, and never has been in our time, any lack of British youths ready to come forward and undergo training for the service. At the same time, it does not seem to have occurred to these persons that British youths are to be found elsewhere than in the British Isles—that is, in Canada, Newfoundland, Australia, and the Cape. If there is anything in this Empire but the name, why should these lads come to England, who desire to join the Navy? Why are there not training-ships at other ports besides Chatham and Plymouth and Portsmouth—at, for example, Halifax, Esquimault, Sydney, and Table Bay?

The answer of the Admiralty to this is that such an innovation would necessitate a great and complicated increase of organisation; that a new and costly system would have to be established, and that the precedent of enlisting colonial boys direct into the service would be used as a precedent for enlisting them direct into the Army by the establishment of recruiting offices at Montreal, Cape Town, and Melbourne. Even then doubt has been expressed, and perhaps rightly, as to the success which would attend such efforts to obtain colonial boys in decent numbers—in countries where there is no surplus population likely to be attracted by such small pecuniary inducements as the Admiralty holds out.

But there is another plan. It is not contended there are not enough men in time of peace. It is the contingency of war which creates the danger. And herein lies all the argument which has been used for the building up and fostering of a great Naval Reserve. In the foregoing pages I have shown that there exists in this one colony of Newfoundland 40,000 loyal, hardy, rugged mariners, who are in a state of enforced idleness for the greater part of the year. These men are Englishmen of the best type—descendants of the sea-dogs of Drake and Hawkins—fearless and stubborn, yet quick to learn, and singularly amenable to discipline. Mr Reid, the contractor, took them from their nets and set them to build the new railway. They were quickly broken in to the work, took their commands from their foreman, and, just as a well-drilled body of bluejackets would build a fort or destroy a rampart, these thousands have accomplished their novel task admirably. There is no doubt about their quality or their quantity. I believe that 10,000 of these enrolled and trained in the Naval Reserve would form as powerful and effective a body of men for purposes of defence as any similar number in the entire British Navy. With an equal, not to say a proportionately larger number drawn from Canada, the difficulty of adequately manning the fleet in time of war is practically disposed of. And it is as well to lay stress upon quality as well as quantity. These men are not weak-chested striplings. There are thousands of youths amongst them, but they are powerfully built, of simple though intelligent character, and accustomed to every species of maritime hardship. They are, in short, of the best type of the old-fashioned British tar. For eight months of the year they are open to enrolment and regular training in the Reserves.

It is not to be expected that the Admiralty will adopt this suggestion immediately; yet that body must be aware that the most pressing need of the Navy is not more ships with more guns, bigger ships with more ingenious armament, but trained men to do the work of the ships already built and building.

The project has already gained the approval of Naval officers who are familiar with the colonial material. The Commander-in-Chief in the Mediterranean, Sir J. O. Hopkins, who recently commanded on the North American station, declares that "if North America will furnish, under suitable regulations, a tithe of its magnificent seafaring population as a Royal Naval Reserve, it will produce a force *in quantity and quality* unsurpassable anywhere."

The proposition is, besides, strongly endorsed by the Premier of Newfoundland, and by the people of that colony themselves. It would be singular—but singularly fitting as well—if the island whose fishing grounds were once the cradle of the English Navy, were at length, after centuries, to furnish new blood and new strength to that same Navy in its need.

APPENDIX

NEWFOUNDLAND AND A NAVAL RESERVE

BY REAR-ADMIRAL LORD CHARLES BERESFORD, C.B.

MANY propositions have lately been put forward with a view to strengthening and augmenting the personnel of the Fleet.

With regard to the colonies in general and Newfoundland in particular providing men for a Naval Reserve, I am a little inclined to doubt the possibility of it under present conditions. In the first place, I do not believe in a Reserve which is vastly inferior in training and quality to the first line. Authority may be right and I may be wrong in regard to the best system of forming a Reserve, but I maintain that any Reserve is practically useless which has not passed through the Fleet or Army to which it forms a Reserve. It must have been trained with the weapons and on the ships it has to man in time of war. Only the most iron discipline, complete training, and confidence in themselves and their officers, will enable men to withstand the brunt of modern naval warfare. It will be bad enough for the first line, but infinitely worse for the Reserve, as they will have to take their places knowing they are filling up losses, and perhaps entrusted with the duty of retrieving disasters.

Every record of history proves that celebrated commanders always chose their best and steadiest men for Reserves. They may, of course, have all been wrong, and authority may be right in thinking that men half-trained and undisciplined will make effective Reserves.

I do not agree with authority on this point, and, therefore, I do not think there is much hope for colonial Reserves of the type of our present Reserves. What I do think possible is, that we shall be able to place training ships at all suitable colonial stations, and there enlist boys and young men for a short service in the British fleet and then discharge them into the Reserve, registering them as Reserve men for mobilisation at certain colonial ports, where modern fast cruisers can be laid up in reserve for these men to man in time of war.

Another point is, that all offers of colonial assistance should come from the colonies first. I am utterly opposed to the Mother Country making the first move. The real test of colonial patriotism will be shown in allowing the colonies to make their own proposals as to what they are willing to do towards Imperial Defence, and then trying to bring their various offers into a concerted form, which will best serve the purpose we all have at heart.

There are two principles which ought to be recognised:

I. The colonies must make the primary advances, and say in effect at what price they value their birthright as British citizens.

II. There must not be a repetition of the Australian principle of contribution, as it would lead to endless complications in time of war, and in the end would be satisfactory neither to the colonies nor ourselves. The colonial contributions should not take the form of ships.

If the colonists of Newfoundland or elsewhere should see their way to raise a Volunteer Naval Reserve, and should offer the control and training of this Reserve to the Admiralty, I certainly think it should be accepted; but I do not think the manning difficulty will be easily overcome by half measures of this sort, and I would rather see such a step as this only supplementary to other efforts. Training the Reserves in the Navy first and then establishing Reserve centres in the colonies, where these men can come up for annual training, would be my plan.

LABRADOR.

IF you want to know what the worst human poverty is like you should try, not London, but Labrador. In the meanest courts and alleys of the world's metropolis there is still a picturesqueness mingled with the squalor, the great chance, the broader outlook, the variety of vicissitude. But in Labrador, amongst Englishmen, it is only dull cold and stupid hunger—large families, much English pluck and pride, a little hope and resolve to make the best of it—and a great deal of gratitude for any attempt to improve their condition.

I have said that the Tenth Island, within her own boundaries, already has more land than she knows what to do with. Yet to the north of her she owns a territory twice as large as herself. Labrador is one of the greatest peninsulas in the world, and the best part of it belongs to Newfoundland. There is a resident white population of some 5000 scattered along the south and east coasts. These people are called "livyeres" (live-heres), and they are all fishermen and their families. To the north of them are the Eskimos, with some Indians, who live by fur-hunting, in the interior.

One cannot help wondering how those 5000 English came to live in Labrador. As one crosses the entrance to the St Lawrence river, the captain invariably points out a treeless, barren island nine miles long and three miles broad.

"That," says he, "is the most desolate spot on God's earth."

It is called on the map Belle Isle; but the "livyeres" and the Eskimos know it as the Isle of Demons, and their legends tell you that if you go near it you will hear a "great clamour of men's voices" wailing and cursing in their agony. There is certainly at times such a noise, but it is probably caused by the crash of small ice-floes.

Some of the "livyeres" are said to be descendants of the men who fled England in the old press-gang days. Others had for ancestors the sailors who were wrecked on the coast; while many others went out in the service of the Hudson Bay Company, which has many trading stations hereabouts. The largest Labrador settlement contains perhaps 350 persons, including the people of the neighbouring coves. But in May or June this coast is visited by as many as 30,000 fishermen, with their families, most of whom are from Newfoundland. One-third of the fishery of the Tenth Island is now done each summer in Labrador—amounting, perhaps, to a million and a half dollars. Yet no lighthouse, buoy, or landmark aid navigation on the Labrador coast. No railway, public building, roads, drains, or such conveniences and institutions exist in Labrador. Every man is a fisherman first, and a mechanic afterwards, for if put to it he can be, and is, boat or house builder, blacksmith, cooper, and curer. No gaol or police are to be found on the land, the sole representative of law and order being a small revenue schooner with a Justice of the Peace on board, who is responsible for maintaining the law and preventing smuggling.

The summer settlements are on islands or outside settlements, and here both Newfoundlanders and "livyeres" dwell, the latter retiring up the bays and inlets, to be nearer wood and game, when the former return to their own homes. There are about a dozen well-recognised central stations in Labrador, where agents of the various St John's merchant firms and others are stationed to collect the fish from the people and ship it thence to market. These agents are the "planters"—the Thomas Codlins of Labrador—who make advances of supplies to the better known of the fishermen, and also employ some of them on wages. Each planter has his own house, but his men usually live together in huts of logs, with the chinks filled with moss and covered with sods. Entrance is by a low doorway, and there is a small window, placed low down to prevent any escape of heat. The families are very prolific, and what is still more remarkable is that the men are tall and broad and muscular—many of them giants. In effect, Labrador is a "land of desolation, with a country hard, relentless, unsympathetic, and cruel, where, among fogs and icebergs, a handful of determined men are trying to hold their own against hostile surroundings and to earn a living in defiance of dreary odds."

And who then is the man who would endeavour, and is endeavouring successfully, to impart some comfort, some brightness, some spiritual sunshine, some material happiness into this land? If ever there was an individual who commanded my admiration and respect, it is Dr Wilfred T. Grenfell. Every Labrador fisherman, woman, and child knows him, and they have his name constantly on their lips. Grenfell is a young Oxford graduate, a surgeon and physician, a priest, an athlete, a master mariner, a Nimrod, a philanthropist, and a brave man. When the Mission to Deep-Sea Fishermen decided to send an expedition to Labrador, it was he who was sent: and what he has done and is now doing for this country and these people, is testified to every day in the week by themselves and their neighbours in the Tenth Island.

"Only a small percentage of the 'livyeres' can read or write," says Dr Grenfell, in his interesting book "Vikings of To-day." "Most school work can be done in winter, for in summer only those too young to work can be spared; and if they are old enough to journey alone to and from the school, they are old enough to do something at the fishery. Only a small percentage can read or write. Every summer it is usual for a Roman Catholic priest, a Methodist minister, and an Anglican clergyman to visit as many stations as they can on the first 400 miles of coast. They are passed along in boats from place to place by the too-willing people, who, irrespective of creed, extend their kindly hospitality to all alike. In places wood buildings have been put up voluntarily by the men in their spare time for Sunday services, conducted usually by one of themselves. Our own gatherings, at times too large for the *Albert's* hold or these little buildings, were held in fish-stores ashore, cleared for the purpose, or in the open air, one of the countless boulders serving for a natural rostrum. I have seen the same place serve in the morning for Church of England, in the afternoon for Wesleyan, in the evening for Salvation Army: and pretty much the same congregation attending each.

"Fresh meat and vegetables are alike hard to procure. No horse or cow exists. The domestic animal world is represented only by the inevitable dog: the vegetable by the stringy cabbage or struggling turnip, whose leaves alone attain to economic value. To prevent scurvy in winter, when fresh fish is not attainable, salt meat must be avoided, even if they can afford to buy it. The following recipe is invented with that end:—'Dry the cod in the sun till it is so hard none can go bad. In winter powder this, rub it up with fresh seal oil, and add cranberries if you have any.' This dainty is known as 'pipsey.' These people neither need nor expect luxuries; sugar and milk are very rarely used, tinned milk being too expensive, molasses being cheaper than sugar, and also margarine than butter. White rabbits, white grouse, and sea-birds help to eke out the winter's diet.

"But, to be accurate, I saw a pig, brought by the Newfoundlanders. When they arrived, the dogs were banished to a desert island near. In another harbour we listened to much wailing. Two pigs had been isolated on an island near, the fishermen enjoying daily the bliss of anticipation. But, alas! here the dogs proved equal to the occasion. An off-shore wind had brought them the joyful news, and that very morning the pigs disappeared, only a few blood-stained bristles remaining to tell the story of the crime. Into one harbour a planter had brought a sheep; but its isolation had so developed its affection for its owner that it followed him everywhere, and he could not make up his mind to kill it."

Until the arrival of the doctors attached to the Mission, no resident surgeon existed in Labrador. No skilled aid was to be obtained in case of need. When sickness fell on the people, no one knew what it was, or how to treat it. Not knowing they were ill, these men used to work on till a trifling ailment became a matter of life and death.

"I sailed on up Stag Bay," writes Dr Grenfell in a letter,

"to visit some settlers. It was dusk when we arrived and pulled our boat up on the beach near the first house. The father and one lad were away. The mother and seven children, the youngest four months old, were at home.

"The house consists of one room, a central cracked stove, two wood bunks, and a porch where the dogs sleep. The woman remarked, 'I am sorry we cannot give you any tea, we have had nothing but flour in the house for more than a month. Richard (her husband) is away selling some seal meat.' They had twelve quintals of fish, two bear skins (one valueless), six sealskins, and a few trout. The seven children were nearly naked. There were seven children, two cotton counterpanes (one for each bed). An exceedingly small kerosene lamp gave us a semi-religious light, and partially veiled the poverty of the surroundings. We cooked some cocoa we had with us, and produced some hard biscuits; but none of them could touch the cocoa because it was sweet, and they were unaccustomed to it. 'Soft loaf' and water had been their 'supper.' One boy, the eldest, tasted the cocoa, and then went out and poured it away. They had not even molasses themselves. We spread our blankets and lay down on the floor. The mother and one child took one bunk, four children the other bunk. Two children lay on the floor. All went to bed with their boots even on—I suppose, for warmth. The stove made the air very close, but we couldn't have the door open because the family had no clothes, so we slept with our heads close to the crack beneath the door for air. We gave this family clothing each year, and last year flour, powder, and molasses as well. Now I have given them an order to cut wood for me, of which there exists plenty all round; also for 'boards,' which I intend to try and send to Long

Tickle to keep some of the superabundant draught out of their prayer meeting house."

"I think," he writes again of a place called Boulter's Rock, "without any exception, I was in the worst human habitation at this place I have ever been in. It beat Connemara hovels and Achill mud houses and West Hebridean crofters' abodes easily. Nor can I attribute it entirely to necessity; for, like many others, the very poorest man having health and strength, as the occupier had, could make it better. Perhaps it is worthy of description. Imagine an ancient and rotten Labrador plank summer-fishing hut, which had been deserted long since by its original occupier, who seemed to have taken his front door and windows with him, while the wintry gales had made adventitious ventilation holes at irregular intervals all over the rest of the building. The present squatter finding the inside too large to co-exist with warmth enough, had pulled down the ceiling, or part thereof, and had roughly divided off one end. Inside was a decrepit stove and a wooden bunk. Two years married, they told me he here spent his whole summer fishing with his wife, who, I must confess, said life was almost intolerable in it. Alongside was half a small hut, well grown over with moss and grass inside, which he was slowly building to accommodate his anticipated family. I need only add that clothes were at a minimum, and food only enough to prevent immediate starvation; and one can form an idea of this hovel, perched on a barren rock over a rough harbour on this Arctic coast."

After all this one wonders why such people continue to live in such a place, especially when the smiling fields of Canada and Western Newfoundland are for their asking. But to the Labradian it is his "ain countree." As Dr

Grenfell says: "The wild life to which these people are born has a certain charm to others besides themselves. Sailors they were born and bred. What else can they do? Some have been taken by the Canadian Government to the southern side of the Gulf of St Lawrence—the Arcady of Longfellow—and yet have found eventually their way back."

Labrador, then, is a colony—and a continually increasing one—of Englishmen.

CURIOUS CASE OF A DOWNING-STREET VETO.

THE remarks of Mr Beckles Willson on the Newfoundland situation, in a recent issue of the *Daily Mail*, to the effect that there appears to be in the minds of the administrators of justice a strong feeling against taking any action which might possibly create unpleasant relations between Great Britain and France, receives a striking confirmation in the case of Captain Cunningham, a gentleman well known in the mining world, who was interviewed yesterday by a *Daily Mail* reporter. In this case the impeding influence of the treaty with France on the industrial development of a very considerable section of Newfoundland is very strongly manifest.

Some years ago Captain Cunningham purchased a number of licences to exploit certain lands, believed to be richly auriferous, situated at Mings Bight, on what is known as the north shore, the coast line of which is within the French limits. Before completing his bargain he consulted Sir William Whiteway, then Attorney-General of the island, and was assured that he ran no risk of interference, as a settlement of the whole question of French rights had been arrived at, and had been sent to the Home Government for confirmation through the usual diplomatic channels. A large number of exceptionally fine specimens of gold quartz was taken to England by Captain Cunningham and exhibited to gentlemen interested in gold mining. As a consequence, an engineer and miners were immediately despatched to Newfoundland. Operations were started in a vigorous manner, prospecting shafts were sunk, and costeans and roads cut through the heavy forest in several directions. Gold was reported to have been found, and the existence of a very powerful band of magnetic iron ore confirmed and traced for a mile or two back from the coast.

"Early in the ensuing summer," said Captain Cunningham, "I visited the workings in order to report progress and take reliable samples of the minerals obtained. I was thus occupied when one morning a French man-o'-war steamed into the Bight, a party of armed bluejackets landed, and planted the French flag over the mouth of the principal shaft. I very naturally demanded of the lieutenant in command an explanation of these high-handed doings, and was by him referred to the admiral, who was on board the man-o'-war.

I promptly interviewed the latter on his ship and was received with the greatest politeness. A copy of the French Treaty was produced, by which I found that work of a permanent character could not be carried on without one half mile of the foreshore, as doing so might possibly interfere with the rights of the French fishermen in preventing them from drying their fish at any point where they might choose to land. In the opinion of the admiral my operations constituted permanent work, although I only used timber in constructing buildings; and that, notwithstanding the fact that no French fishermen ever plied their trade in these parts, still he had no option in the matter.

"It was impossible for me to go behind this treaty, as you may imagine; so, practically shutting down the mines, I took the first mail boat for England. The admiral, who was courtesy itself, had advised me to go to Paris and endeavour to come to an understanding with the French Government. He would further the business by his personal recommendations, as he regretted having had to stop our work, even temporarily. Before leaving St John's the admiral gave me an introduction to his immediate chief, the Minister of Marine, as a first step towards a useful solution of the difficulty.

"Unfortunately for myself, I stopped in London on my way to Paris, and conferred at Downing Street with the Secretary for Foreign Affairs, and to my dismay, a peremptory veto was put on my visit to the French Minister of Marine. I was told it would be considered an interference, and prejudicial to the success of the diplomatic negotiations then going on. I was led to infer that if I persisted and succeeded with the French Government, the British authorities would not recognise such modifications as were necessary, and would prevent their application to my case."

"The amount," concluded Captain Cunningham, "that was sunk in my property was not far from £20,000, which is as utterly lost as if I had thrown it into the sea. If I had been permitted to go on with the work, I am certain that it would have proved a valuable concern; but as the matter stands, I have bitter cause to rue Downing Street's 'fear of unpleasant relations.'"—From the London *Daily Mail*, January 1st, 1897.

www.ingramcontent.com/pod-product-compliance
Lightning Source LLC
Chambersburg PA
CBHW021838230426
43669CB00008B/1005